AF601291

# *The* GINGERBREAD PARTY

# *The* GINGERBREAD PARTY

## *Recipes and Traditions for Christmas Entertaining*

Courtney Dial Whitmore
WITH Phronsie Dial
Photographs by CAMERON WILDER

Gibbs Smith

First Edition
30 29 28 27 26 5 4 3 2 1



Published by
Gibbs Smith
570 N. Sportsplex Dr.
Kaysville, Utah 84037
www.gibbs-smith.com
The authorized representative in the EEA is Simon and Schuster Netherlands BV, Herculesplein 96 3584 AA Utrecht, Netherlands, info@simonandschuster.nl

Designed by Sheryl Dickert and Renee Bond
Printed and bound in China

Library of Congress Control Number: 2025946583
ISBN: 978-1-4236-6912-8
Ebook ISBN: 978-1-4236-6913-5

This product is made of FSC®-certified and other controlled material.

*For Ivy and Blakely:*
*May you always find a little magic*
*in candy rooftops, fluffy swirls of icing,*
*and every gingerbread memory we've made together.*
*And when you're grown, may these pages bring you home.*

# CONTENTS

# INTRODUCTION

*Christmas waves a magic wand over this world, and behold, everything is softer and more beautiful.*

—Norman Vincent Peale

My mother has always been the queen of gingerbread houses. My earliest Christmas memories are of my mother sitting at the dining room table, piping fluffy royal icing onto charming little houses, ready to be bagged as favors for a tea party or brought to school for a classroom holiday party. She has hosted elegant gingerbread house tea parties for decades, inviting moms and daughters to celebrate the season with gingerbread houses, sipping spiced tea from silver teacups, and leaving with hearts full. Her very first Christmas tea party? It was held in December 1984, just a month after I was born. And the tradition still continues.

Believe it or not, we still hear from dear friends who've carefully preserved those early gingerbread houses, tucked away in airtight bags and displayed each December on mantels and tabletops. Yes, you can absolutely save these little houses (with the occasional candy renovation, of course). While we gift new ones, they love the cherished memories of those old houses.

When I became a mother, it was a joy to carry on this beloved Christmas tradition, beginning when my older daughter was just two. Since she and her friends were still quite young, we decorated one large gingerbread house together and donated it to a local children's nonprofit. By the time they turned three, each little girl was ready to decorate her own. Now, with two daughters by my side, we continue to host our pink-and-peppermint dream of a gathering each year complete with fluffy royal icing, candy-cane details, sugar-dusted tablescapes, and the gingerbread houses that started it all, always finished with a bow on top!

Over the years, it's been the sweetest surprise to watch this little tradition travel far and wide. We've received photos and messages from readers around the world—yes, even from England

and France—who've hosted their own gingerbread celebrations inspired by the parties we shared online. For years, we've been asked to create a book with every recipe, tip, and detail.

So here it is: *The Gingerbread Party*.

Inside these pages, you'll find all the sweet inspiration you need to start a gingerbread tradition of your own. It is jam-packed with decorating tutorials, Christmas recipes, hosting tips, and plenty of party ideas, not just for little girls' teas but also for train-loving boys, ladies' nights, cozy family gatherings, classroom celebrations, and gift-giving moments too.

Whether you're throwing a gingerbread party, helping out with a school celebration, or just decorating houses with your children or grandchildren around the kitchen table, I hope these pages spark a little inspiration. Don't stress about perfect piping or competition-worthy houses. We believe every gingerbread house deserves a little whimsy and charm, slightly lopsided rooftops and crooked chimneys included. No two are alike, and that's exactly how it should be.

Wherever and however you celebrate, I hope these gingerbread traditions, recipes, and ideas bring as much joy to your season as they have to ours. Merry Christmas!

*The best holiday gifts aren't bought from a store.*
*They're handmade, piped with icing, and finished with a bow on top.*

Courtney & [illegible]

# HISTORY OF GINGERBREAD

*An I had but one penny in the world,*
*thou should'st have it to buy ginger-bread.*

—William Shakespeare, *Love's Labour's Lost* (Act 5, Scene 1)

The history of gingerbread is a story that begins not with sugar, but with spice. Ancient Chinese farmers first grew ginger, which then traveled along spice routes to the West. Cherished for its bold flavor and believed healing properties, ginger eventually found its way into sweet treats. One of the earliest gingerbread-like recipes dates back to around 2400 BC in ancient Greece, made with honey and spices. But it was medieval Europe that truly embraced gingerbread.

By the Middle Ages, it was the star of "Gingerbread Fairs" across England, France, and Germany. Bakers pressed gingerbread dough into carved wooden molds shaped like hearts, animals, and knights, then decorated them with icing or gold leaf.

Queen Elizabeth I brought gingerbread into the royal spotlight, famously commissioning cookies shaped like visiting dignitaries and members of her court. Carefully piped and sometimes gilded, these edible portraits served as both flattery and entertainment at court.

Fast-forward to 1812, when the Brothers Grimm enchanted readers with *Hansel and Gretel* and their iconic candy-covered cottage. In Germany, elaborate gingerbread houses, called *Lebkuchenhäuschen*, became a cherished holiday custom. Around the same time, Queen Victoria and Prince Albert helped establish gingerbread as a Christmas tradition. Drawing on Albert's German heritage and love for decorated sweets, they paired gingerbread with Christmas trees and handmade ornaments.

From ancient spice routes to royal courts to fairy-tale forests, gingerbread has long been more than just a sweet treat. From decorating houses with your kids to swapping cookies with neighbors, each moment carries a bit of the magic that's made gingerbread a beloved tradition for centuries.

# THE ART OF MAKING GINGERBREAD

In the pages that follow, you'll find six chapters full of gingerbread ideas. They're arranged to guide you through parties, projects, and recipes with step-by-step tutorials, helpful tips, and personal stories woven throughout. There's no right or wrong place to start, but be *sure* not to skip these notes on tools, tips, and tricks below.

## Essential Tools and Materials

Before you begin baking and building, it's helpful to have the right tools on hand. Some are truly essential, others just make the process a little easier (or more fun). Some are must-haves for all gingerbread projects, while others are specific to cut-and-bake builds like houses, sleighs, and wreaths.

### RECOMMENDED FOR ALL PROJECTS

These basics apply whether you're building with graham crackers or homemade gingerbread.

- Baking sheets
- Electric mixer (for royal icing and dough prep, hand or stand mixer)
- Parchment paper or silicone baking mats (such as Silpat)
- Paring knife (for cutting dough or fine trimming)
- Pastry bags (or ziplock bags in a pinch)
- Piping tips (round and star tips are the most versatile; we most often use 1M, 4B, 32, 21, 3, and 2)

### RECOMMENDED FOR BAKED GINGERBREAD PROJECTS

Essential if you're creating custom shapes like houses, wreaths, or sleighs.

- Pencil or fine-tip marker (to label and mark template pieces)
- Plastic wrap (for wrapping and chilling dough)
- Poster board or card stock (to create reusable templates)
- Ruler or measuring tape (for accurate measuring and cutting)
- Rolling pin (for gingerbread dough)
- Small knife or X-Acto (for clean, sharp cuts around template edges)

### RECOMMENDED FOR GRAHAM CRACKER HOUSES

- Ruler (for measuring uniform cuts)
- Serrated knife (for trimming graham crackers)

### HELPFUL EXTRAS

Not required, but handy for decorating, detail work, or smoothing after baking.

- Bowl scraper (for handling dough or cleaning surfaces)
- Cooling racks (for airflow and even drying)
- Plastic storage containers or tote bins (for protecting finished pieces from dust and curious hands)
- Gelatin sheets (for "glass" windows)
- Hot glue gun and glue sticks (especially for graham cracker houses and attaching decorations—choose a strong-hold glue stick such as Gorilla Hot Glue Sticks)
- Microplane or fine grater (for trimming uneven edges)
- Offset spatula (for lifting delicate pieces and spreading icing)
- Small paintbrush (for brushing off flour)

## Before You Begin: Smart Baking Tips

A few helpful reminders before you dive in, gathered from years of trial, error, and many batches of gingerbread.

## TEMPLATES AND SHAPING

- Use poster board or card stock for templates. Take your time and label each piece so you know how many to cut. You can reuse them again.
- Keep a dedicated envelope or folder to store all your templates from year to year. I like to group them by project and label them (Classic House, Sleigh, Wreath, etc.) so they're easy to grab when it's time to build.

## WORKING WITH DOUGH

- Use unsulfured molasses—not blackstrap or sulfured molasses, which are too bitter.
- Roll large pieces of dough between sheets of parchment paper or directly onto a silicone baking mat (our personal preference). Cut your shapes, then peel away excess dough and transfer the whole mat to your baking sheet.
- Lightly flour your surface, rolling pin, and dough as needed. Re-flour periodically to prevent sticking. I keep a small bowl of flour by my work surface and use it often.
- If using cutters, dip them in flour before pressing into the dough.
- Extra dough? Wrap tightly in plastic wrap. Store in the refrigerator for up to 3 days.

## BAKING TIPS

- Gingerbread will be slightly soft when it comes out of the oven. Let it rest a few minutes; it will firm as it cools. If any piece feels too soft after cooling, return it to the oven for 2 to 3 minutes more.
- Always let your gingerbread pieces cool completely before moving or icing.
- I like to bake pieces a day or two before decorating so they're nice and firm.
- Oven temperatures vary. Bake similar-sized pieces together, or remove smaller pieces early and return larger pieces to finish baking.

## FOR GRAHAM CRACKER PROJECTS

- When attaching graham crackers to the box base, we use hot glue. Gorilla Hot Glue Sticks are our go-tos for strength and hold.
- Cutting graham crackers? Use a small serrated knife and a gentle sawing motion on a flat surface to score and snap cleanly. Don't rush; going slow helps prevent breakage.
- Buy an extra box! Graham crackers break easily, so having spares on hand will save you the stress of running out mid-project.

## Baking in Humid Climates

- **Let baked pieces sit out overnight before assembling.** Allow your gingerbread to rest uncovered for several hours or overnight so the pieces firm up fully before you begin decorating, especially in humid climates.
- **Dry your pieces in the driest room possible.** Choose a space away from moisture and avoid dishwashers, stovetops, and running laundry. An air-conditioned room helps keep humidity low so pieces dry evenly.
- **Avoid assembling on rainy days if possible.** High outdoor humidity can sneak inside, so wait for a dry day if you're planning an elaborate build.
- **Pipe the royal icing borders for stability.** We recommend piping the thick royal icing borders within a few days of assembling your house or project. The weight and firmness of the royal icing borders adds important structural support, especially if any softening occurs in humid environments.
- **Storing the finished pieces.** After piping the royal icing borders, we set our gingerbread houses on high surfaces to keep them safe from curious hands (or paws). A gingerbread train *did* mysteriously disappear during the making of this book—because yes, dogs love gingerbread too. Once your house or other gingerbread project is completely dry, store it in a plastic bin to keep it safe and moisture-free until the party. Just be sure not to seal the bin too soon, as moisture can get trapped inside. Because we pipe a thick-bordered royal icing, we allow at least a week of drying time before sealing the houses in a bin.

## Fix-It Guide: Common Gingerbread Issues

### UNEVEN OR WARPED PIECES AFTER BAKING?

As soon as the baked gingerbread pieces come out of the oven, gently place a large sheet pan or baking rack on top to help flatten any puffed or curled areas.

### DOUGH TOO SOFT TO TRANSFER CUTOUT SHAPES?

Roll and cut shapes directly on parchment paper or a silicone baking mat, peel away the excess dough, and transfer the entire parchment sheet or mat to your baking sheet. This keeps windows, doors, and small pieces from stretching or tearing.

### CUTOUT DETAILS LOSING THEIR SHARPNESS?

If your dough has gotten too warm, chill the dough (or cutouts on the pan if you've already cut them) in the refrigerator for 5 to 10 minutes before baking to help preserve the shape while they bake.

### ROYAL ICING NOT HOLDING HEAVY GINGERBREAD PIECES TOGETHER?

Use stiff royal icing for assembly. If in doubt, test it. When you lift your spoon, it should hold a firm peak. Let each section of your gingerbread house dry fully before moving on to the next. It may take more than one day for assembly.

### PIECES SHIFTING WHILE DRYING?

Use mugs, cans, and other household items to prop walls and roofs in place as they set. Don't rush. Make sure each gingerbread house section is fully secure before continuing to build.

### EDGES SLIGHTLY UNEVEN AFTER BAKING?

Once cooled, gently use a Microplane or fine grater to smooth out crumbs and trim warped sides. It's a quick way to get cleaner seams and snug fits.

## Building Gingerbread Creations

At first glance, building a gingerbread house (or sleigh, or wreath!) might feel a little overwhelming, but trust us, once you break it down, it becomes a manageable process. The key is giving yourself time, reading through each recipe, and approaching it step-by-step. You'll learn that there's a gingerbread project for every skill level.

### QUICK-START OVERVIEW

**Step 1:** Choose your design and review the template measurements.

**Step 2:** Read through the full recipe and gather your ingredients and tools. Be sure you've read through the Fix-It Guide on the previous page.

**Step 3:** Bake, cool, and build. Let each step fully dry before moving on.

**Step 4:** Decorate and enjoy!

If you're short on time or working with little ones, graham cracker houses are a fantastic shortcut.

In an even bigger hurry? Store-bought kits are a perfectly fine starting point. Just replace the kit icing with our Gingerbread House Royal Icing (page 41) for a sturdier, more reliable hold.

## Decorating Gingerbread Projects

### BEST CANDIES FOR DECORATING

Over the years, we've learned (the hard way) that not all candies are cut out for gingerbread decorating, especially in humid climates. Traditional peppermints and candy canes may look darling at first, but they tend to "drool" their red coloring over time (we still use them occasionally, just with caution).

Experience has taught us which candies hold up beautifully for the entire holiday season. Here are some of our favorites:

- Butter mints—Soft pastel colors for a vintage cottage look
- Candy buttons (on paper)—Retro and playful
- Chocolate rocks—Perfect for chimneys, landscaping, or fireplaces
- Cinnamon red hots—Tiny and spicy, perfect for wreath berries or accents
- Coconut—Shredded coconut is great for adding snow-like texture
- Fruit slice chews—Cut into mini wedges for fruity shingles
- Gumballs—Big, bold, and fun (try them on rooftops or candy fences)
- Gumdrops (large and small)—Great for trees, garden borders, or candy bushes, cut in half for decorating small spaces
- Jellybeans—Bright pops of color
- Jordan almonds—Smooth and shiny, great for pathways or roof accents
- M&M's—Classic choice for borders or just about anywhere
- Marshmallows—Stack as snowmen or use as fluffy roof "snow"
- Mini gingerbread men cookies—Add to the yard or porch like tiny guests
- Necco Wafers—Ideal for tiled roofs or stone walkways
- Peppermint sticks—Use for porch posts, doorframes, or railings
- Pretzel sticks—Rustic railings, fences, or mini logs
- Rock candy—Sparkly icicles or sugar crystal snow
- Sprinkles (all shapes and colors)—Use everywhere for festive flair

- Sugar decorations—Found in the baking aisle, these tiny themed accents (like wreaths, snowflakes, or Santa hats) are a favorite
- Sugar pearls or dragées—Tiny ornaments or garland trim

## SUGARING FRUIT AND HERBS

This simple technique is perfect for coating small fruits and herbs like cranberries, rosemary sprigs, or even mint with a sparkling, snowy finish. For whole fruits like lemons, limes, and oranges, use the same method but with light corn syrup to help the sugar cling. These sugared fruits make gorgeous holiday décor, whether displayed in a bowl, tucked onto a mantel, or arranged into topiaries.

1. **Make simple syrup:** Heat ½ cup sugar and ½ cup water in a small saucepan until sugar dissolves. Let cool slightly. Short on time? You can also use store-bought simple syrup.
2. **Dip:** Toss fruit or herb sprigs in the syrup to coat. Use a fork to lift them out, letting excess simple syrup drip off.
3. **Roll in sugar:** Roll the fruit or herb sprigs in granulated sugar (or coarse sparkling sugar) until coated.
4. **Dry:** Spread on parchment paper and let dry for about 1 hour. For extra sparkle, dip and sugar them a second time to build a thicker, frostier coating.

## NONEDIBLE FINISHING TOUCHES

While there's certainly something special about a completely edible gingerbread creation, we also believe there's room for a little creative license! For houses and other gingerbread projects meant to be admired rather than eaten, a few nonedible touches, like a velvet bow, a miniature wreath, or a tiny craft-store Santa, can add charm and character. Whether you choose to keep it entirely edible or add a few festive extras, it's all about creating something that feels uniquely yours!

- **Ribbon:** We love to add a big bow on top of each gingerbread house! It's our signature finish. Keep extra ribbon on hand to tie around chimneys and wreaths or create tiny bows to hand out for kids to use on their own houses.
- **Mini ornaments and figurines:** The holiday aisle at the local craft store is full of treasures. Look for miniature snowmen, candy canes, Santas, and other seasonal figurines to tuck into scenes. We've even been known to add a favorite princess or toy soldier at the request of our youngest little decorators.
- **Tiny trees, garlands, and wreaths:** Bottlebrush trees, felt garlands, or mini pine wreaths can also add charm.

# HOW TO START YOUR OWN GINGERBREAD PARTY TRADITION

You don't need a big guest list or a picture-perfect setup to start a meaningful tradition. All it takes is a little gingerbread, a few bowls of candy, and a whole lot of holiday spirit. Here's how to get started:

- **Start small:** Invite a couple of friends over, turn on the Christmas music, and get decorating.
- **Choose your "house":** Whether it's classic gingerbread houses, simple graham cracker houses, gingerbread trains, sleighs, or more, you'll find all the recipes and tutorials you need inside these pages.
- **Build early:** We actually build our graham cracker houses in August! Prepping the bases and piping on the royal icing borders well before the holiday rush keeps December a little less hectic. Built and stored properly, they'll be ready to go when it's time to party. We recommend large plastic bins with tops to secure them. Store in a cool, dry area.
- **Prep ahead:** Set your table a few days, or even a week, in advance so you have time to gather candies, shop for royal icing ingredients, and fine-tune the details at your own pace.
- **Set the scene:** Whether you're hosting a children's tea party or a grown-up gathering, create a festive mood with ribbons, twinkling lights, florals, and special holiday touches like nutcrackers and sprigs of fresh greenery.
- **Make it personal:** Add place cards, pipe guests' names on a cookie-shaped house, or send everyone home with a mini house party favor. There's no wrong way to do it.
- **Repeat annually:** That's the magic. What begins as a little seasonal fun turns into a beloved tradition your guests, and especially your children, will look forward to every single year.

*The*

# GINGERBREAD HOUSE TEA PARTY

*Where peppermint dreams and pink holiday magic come to life!*

Step inside these pages for a glimpse into our annual Gingerbread House Tea Party, an enchanting tradition sprinkled with pink peppermint, marshmallows, and Sugar Plum Fairy dreams. My mother hosted gingerbread house parties for me growing up, and it's been one of my greatest joys to continue the celebration with my own daughters. They love inviting friends to kick off the season with this special gathering. One year, my younger daughter even took her very first steps right in the middle of the party.

As our little "decorators" arrive, they're greeted by a pair of four-foot pink nutcrackers at the front door and a gingerbread wreath that hints at the magic to come. Inside, a Christmas tree sparkles with miniature gingerbread houses tucked among the branches. Each girl's place is set with her ready-to-decorate house and a cake stand holding a miniature gingerbread house to take home, perfect for a favorite doll or teddy bear.

A long child-size table dressed in soft pink gingham sets the stage. At each place, a peppermint place mat and a paper plate (perfect for catching stray sprinkles and icing drips) are accompanied by the sweetest gingerbread house napkins. Tied to the backs of each chair, red satin bows and mini stockings bring extra cheer to the table.

Down the center of the table, you'll find a whimsical procession of pink nutcrackers—some tall, some tiny—collected over the years for my girls. Between them: vases of red and pink roses, pastel ceramic trees, and a grand gingerbread house centerpiece. Scattered among the flowers and figurines, strands of fairy lights weave through small glass bowls and baking cups filled with candies: pink butter mints, gumdrops, red hots, pastel chocolate nonpareils, jelly beans, and pink-and-white marshmallows.

Over the years, this party has sparked joy not just in our home but in many others as well. Readers have created their own versions and shared sweet photos from around the world.

If you're dreaming up a Gingerbread House Tea Party of your own, know it can be as elaborate or as simple as you'd like. Whether you borrow a few ideas or follow every detail, the real magic happens when the music is playing, the sugar is flying, and the table is full of smiling faces.

# Gingerbread Cupcakes with Vanilla Buttercream

*Topped with tiny spiced cookie row houses, these gingerbread cupcakes are a delight to make and eat!*

MAKES 12 STANDARD CUPCAKES

## GINGERBREAD CUPCAKES

1 ½ cups all-purpose flour

1 teaspoon baking powder

¼ teaspoon baking soda

½ teaspoon salt

2 ½ teaspoons ground cinnamon

2 teaspoons ground ginger

½ teaspoon ground cloves

¼ teaspoon ground nutmeg

6 tablespoons unsalted butter, softened to room temperature

¾ cup packed light brown sugar

½ cup unsulfured molasses

¼ cup vegetable oil

2 large eggs

1 teaspoon vanilla extract

¾ cup buttermilk, room temperature

Preheat the oven to 350 degrees F. Line a standard cupcake pan with cupcake liners.

In a medium bowl, whisk together the flour, baking powder, baking soda, salt, cinnamon, ginger, cloves, and nutmeg. Set aside.

In the bowl of a stand mixer fitted with the paddle attachment, cream the softened butter and brown sugar on medium speed until light and fluffy, 2 to 3 minutes.

Add the molasses and vegetable oil, mixing until thoroughly combined. Scrape down the sides of the bowl as needed.

Beat in the eggs, one at a time, then add the vanilla.

With the mixer on low speed, add half of the dry ingredients, then the buttermilk, followed by the remaining dry ingredients. Mix until just combined. Do not overmix.

Divide the batter evenly among the prepared cupcake liners, filling each about ⅔ full.

Bake for 16 to 18 minutes, or until a toothpick inserted into the center comes out clean or with a few moist crumbs.

Cool the cupcakes completely before frosting.

*Continued*

### VANILLA BUTTERCREAM FROSTING

1 cup (2 sticks) unsalted butter, softened to room temperature

3 to 4 cups powdered sugar

¼ teaspoon salt

1 tablespoon vanilla extract

3 tablespoons milk or heavy cream

In the bowl of a stand mixer fitted with the paddle attachment, beat the butter on medium speed for 2 minutes, until smooth and creamy.

Reduce the speed to low and gradually add the powdered sugar, 1 cup at a time, mixing until fully incorporated.

Add the salt, vanilla, and milk. Increase speed to medium and beat for 3 minutes, until light and fluffy.

If the frosting is too thick, add additional milk, 1 tablespoon at a time. Add more powdered sugar, 2 tablespoons at a time, for a firmer consistency.

## Spice Cookie Row Houses (Cupcake Topper)

*These tall, narrow spice cookies are trimmed and decorated to resemble festive little row houses, each one finished with piped royal icing and colorful sprinkles. Whether they remind you of Charleston single houses or a snowy stretch of holiday brownstones, they make a charming topper for gingerbread cupcakes. You can also serve them on their own as a holiday treat, or package them as sweet little favors for guests to take home.*

### YOU'LL NEED:

Biscoff cookies (or similar rectangular tea cookies)

Gingerbread House Royal Icing—Follow the recipe on page 41, but instead of 5 cups of powdered sugar, use 3 to 4 cups. This will produce a thinner icing for piping tiny details with small piping tips but still hardens to the touch.

Sprinkles, candies, or nonpareils for decorating

Tiny ribbon bows (remove before eating), optional

### INSTRUCTIONS:

1. Flip the cookies over so the flat sides face up.
2. Using a serrated knife, carefully trim the top corners to form a roof shape.
3. Outline and decorate the cookies with royal icing, adding sprinkles or candies as desired. Pipe a tiny ribbon bow on top or add a nonedible ribbon bow for a finishing touch.
4. Let the icing set completely before placing the cookies upright into frosted cupcakes.
5. Garnish each cupcake with a small sprig of sugared rosemary for a festive, wintry touch.

# Crispy Pimento Cheese Cups

*These festive little toast cups are a must at all of our parties. Even guests who think they're not fans of pimento cheese are quickly converted after tasting one right from the oven.*

MAKES 36 CUPS

### PIMENTO CHEESE

2 cups grated sharp cheddar cheese

1 (4-ounce) jar diced pimientos

1 cup high-quality mayonnaise (like Duke's)

⅛ teaspoon salt

¼ teaspoon hot pepper sauce or 1 jalapeño pepper, finely chopped

### CRISPY TOAST CUPS

1 loaf thinly sliced sandwich bread

½ cup butter, softened

Diced chives, for garnish

In a large bowl, combine the grated cheese, pimientos with their liquid, mayonnaise, salt, and hot pepper sauce. Stir until well mixed. Cover and chill for at least 2 hours.

Preheat the oven to 350 degrees F.

Using a rolling pin, roll each slice of bread slightly and use a 2-inch biscuit cutter or cookie cutter to cut out two rounds from each slice. Each loaf of bread has about 18 slices, not using the end slices. After cutting the bread rounds, brush the inside of a mini muffin pan with butter. Carefully fit the bread rounds into the mini muffin pan. Brush the inside of the bread rounds with butter. Bake the empty cups for 10 minutes. Remove from oven and fill the cups with the pimento cheese mixture. Bake again for 5 to 7 minutes. Garnish with diced chives.

These cups are twice baked, making them very crispy and delicious. Toasted cups, before being filled, can also be frozen to be filled and baked at a later time.

*Tip:* Crispy toast cups can be used for a variety of hors d'oeuvres. Fill them with anything from chicken salad to spinach artichoke dip for a delicious party bite.

# Christmas Party Fruit Tea

*This Christmas party tea is fruity, lightly spiced, and just right for little teacups. While technically no actual tea is involved, we've been serving this whimsical fruit "tea" for years at our gingerbread house parties.*

SERVES 24 (4-OUNCES EACH)

1 quart apple juice

1 quart pineapple juice

1 quart orange juice

Cinnamon sticks, orange slices, and fresh cranberries, for garnish

In a large punch bowl, combine the apple, pineapple, and orange juices. Add a few cinnamon sticks, orange slices, and a handful of cranberries to float on top for a festive touch. Serve chilled or warm in small teacups.

*Tip:* To turn this into a festive adult punch, add 1 to 1½ cups of spiced rum or vodka to the chilled mixture before serving.

# Christmas Chocolate Fudge

*My godmother Jayne's recipe for chocolate fudge was passed down from her grandmother in Virginia. We gift it to neighbors and friends each year, and it always finds its way onto a Christmas platter at our Gingerbread House Tea Party. It's a holiday staple. And you read it right: 3 full tablespoons of vanilla extract.*

MAKES 100 SQUARES

4 ½ cups sugar

1 (12-ounce) can evaporated milk

4 teaspoons cornstarch

3 cups semisweet chocolate chips

1 cup unsalted butter, room temperature

3 tablespoons vanilla extract

1 ½ cups chopped pecans, toasted, optional

Combine the sugar, milk, and cornstarch in a large saucepan over medium heat. Bring mixture to a boil, stirring continuously. Once a rolling boil is reached, allow to continue boiling for 6 minutes, stirring frequently. Remove from the heat and stir in chocolate chips, butter, and vanilla until well combined. If using the pecans, add them now and stir well. Quickly spread mixture into a 9 x 13-inch baking pan lined with parchment paper and allow to cool. Refrigerate to speed up the cooling process. After fudge has cooled, lift out of pan using the ends of parchment paper and cut into 1-inch squares.

*Tip:* Place fudge squares in foil candy wrappers for a pretty presentation.

# Chocolate Fudge Cakelets

*These rich, chocolatey cakelets have earned their permanent place at our annual Gingerbread House Tea Party. They're my older daughter's favorite, so my mother never fails to set out a silver platter piled high with them on the dining room table, and they're always the first to disappear. We love a from-scratch recipe, but this one begins with a simple cake mix and ends up as one of the best things you'll ever put in your mouth. Don't say I didn't warn you when the platter vanishes.*

MAKES 90 TO 96 CAKELETS

1 box chocolate cake mix

1 small box instant chocolate pudding

1 cup sour cream

½ cup vegetable oil

½ cup lukewarm water

4 large eggs, room temperature

2 cups miniature semisweet chocolate chips

Preheat the oven to 350 degrees F. In the bowl of a stand mixer fitted with the paddle attachment (or in a large mixing bowl if using an electric hand mixer), combine the chocolate cake mix, instant chocolate pudding, sour cream, vegetable oil, lukewarm water, and eggs. Beat on medium speed for about 5 minutes, stopping to scrape down the sides of the bowl as needed. Stir in the chocolate chips until evenly distributed.

Lightly spray a miniature muffin pan with nonstick baking spray. Fill each cup of the pan with 1 tablespoon of batter. Bake for 11 to 13 minutes, or until the tops spring back lightly when touched. Cool completely before icing. If preparing in advance, freeze the cakelets (unfrosted) until ready to thaw and ice.

## FUDGE ICING

1 cup (2 sticks) butter (we use salted, but either will do)

3 cups sugar

⅔ cup evaporated milk

1 cup semisweet chocolate chips

In a heavy saucepan over medium heat, combine the butter, sugar, and evaporated milk. Continue stirring until a rolling boil begins. Let boil for 1 minute, then remove from the heat and stir in the chocolate chips until melted. Spoon warm fudge icing over each cakelet. This icing sets quickly, so work quickly. If needed, return the pan to low heat and stir to keep it smooth.

The cakelets freeze beautifully, but the icing does not, so plan to ice them the day before or the day of your party.

*Party Tip:* We absolutely adore this chocolate cake recipe and often bake it in a Bundt pan for birthdays, holidays, and all kinds of celebrations. To make it as a Bundt cake, prepare the batter as directed and pour it into a greased Bundt pan. Bake at 350 degrees F for 50 to 60 minutes, or until a toothpick inserted in the center comes out clean.

# Graham Cracker Gingerbread House Tutorial

*These sweet graham cracker houses are where it all began. My mom started making them years ago, using little milk cartons as the base, an easy and sturdy foundation. While they're not made with actual gingerbread, they're every bit a gingerbread house in spirit and charm. Year after year, these darling houses steal the show at our Gingerbread House Tea Party.*

Since it's very difficult to make a house and decorate it in the same day, we build (and pipe the borders of the houses) in advance so the girls can jump right into the fun of decorating without worrying about a roof collapse.

> *Tip:* For an easy shortcut, look online for premade house-shaped cardboard bases to build the graham cracker houses. Just be sure to choose ones made from sturdy cardboard.

### MAKING THE BOX BASE

**1. Start with a Box:** Use a small cardboard box as the base for the house. For our annual party, we use a 4 x 4-inch box. Any small, sturdy box works. Keep in mind, the finished house will be larger once you add the graham crackers, roof, and icing.

**2. Create the Roof:** Cut a piece of cardboard into a 6 x 12-inch rectangle. Score and fold it in half to form a peaked roof shape. Hot glue it on top of the box, leaving about a 1-inch overhang on each side.

**3. Add End Triangles:** Cut two cardboard triangles to fill in the open gaps on each end of the roof. For a 4 x 4-inch box, the triangles we cut are usually about 4½ inches wide at the base and 5½ inches tall on both sides (measured from the base to the roof peak). Trim as needed so they fit snugly. Glue the triangles into place underneath the roofline to close up each end. Don't worry about perfection; Gingerbread House Royal Icing (page 41) and graham crackers will cover everything beautifully!

### A NOTE ON BOX SIZE

A 3 x 3-inch box also works well for a smaller house. Simply adjust the roof and triangle measurements accordingly. You can also experiment with taller rectangular boxes or shorter, wider ones to create different house shapes. The possibilities are endless! See our Mini Graham Cracker Houses Tutorial on page 42.

## COVERING THE BOX BASE WITH GRAHAM CRACKERS

Use regular honey graham crackers to cover the sides of the cardboard house. Be sure to have plenty of graham crackers so grab an extra box or two just in case you have breakage or need extras.

Carefully cut the crackers to fit each side of the house. To do this, score the cracker using a gentle sawing motion with a serrated knife, then break along the line. Don't worry if a few crack. That's part of the process!

We usually skip adding graham crackers to the roof since it gets fully coated in fluffy royal icing. But if you prefer, you can use the same scoring and breaking technique to cover the roof with graham crackers too.

## PIPING THE ICING ON THE HOUSES

**Piped Bottom Base (Optional):** This step adds a raised, decorative icing border that lifts the house slightly, but you can skip it if you prefer the house to sit flush. After all the graham crackers are glued to the sides of the house, turn the house upside down and place it in a bowl or container that will hold it steady in that position. This gives you easy access to the bottom edges.

Using a batch of our Gingerbread House Royal Icing (page 41) and a large star tip (such as a 1M), pipe along all four bottom edges of the house to create a fluffy, snow-like trim. You can use a piping bag or a frosting tube, whichever you prefer. Allow icing to dry overnight.

**Pipe Remaining Edges:** The next day, flip each house right side up. Pipe royal icing along all the remaining edges (roofline and all edges of the house). Let the royal icing dry and harden overnight before decorating or preparing to store for a later party. A completely dry base makes decorating so much easier for kids.

## DECORATING DAY: FINAL ICING TOUCHES

When we host our gingerbread house parties, we like to set up each finished house at the guests' place settings so they're ready for decorating when they arrive.

Thirty minutes to one hour before party time, we spread our Gingerbread House Royal Icing on both sides of each house's roof and immediately add sprinkles while it's still wet. (Since sprinkles go everywhere, do this step over a trash can or sink for quick cleanup.) The icing on the roofs creates the perfect snowy base for decorating. Don't prepare this step too far ahead of time. The icing should still be soft when decorating begins so the children can press candies into the roof.

Next, we fill frosting tubes with Gingerbread House Royal Icing and pipe large, fluffy swirls along the sides of the house, creating doors and windows, as the kids decorate. If your decorators are a bit older, they can handle their own frosting tubes; we keep a dozen on hand and reuse them each year. You can also use large piping bags.

Once the houses are finished, we send them home in handled cardboard tray boxes for easy transport. Parents can gently adjust any candy that may have shifted during the ride home. The icing will fully harden overnight, and everything will be firmly set and ready to save and display for years to come.

## HOW MUCH ICING WILL I NEED?

Whether you're making one house or a dozen, it helps to plan ahead. These sweet little houses use more Gingerbread House Royal Icing than you might expect! If your houses are roughly the same size as ours, use the following guide. You'll be making the Gingerbread House Royal Icing in stages to allow the earlier piping to dry before moving on.

## TO MAKE 6 GRAHAM CRACKER HOUSES

**Day 1: Pipe the Bottom Borders**—Make one batch of Gingerbread House Royal Icing. One batch will pipe the bottom edges of six or seven houses.

**Day 2: Pipe the Sides and Roofline**—Flip the houses upright. One batch of Gingerbread House Royal Icing will pipe the sides and rooflines of 1½ houses, so plan to work in double batches.

- A double batch will pipe about three houses.
- For six houses, make a second double batch to finish the remaining three.
- The Gingerbread House Royal Icing recipe doubles beautifully in a standard electric mixer, but a triple batch is too large, so stick with single or double batches only. When in doubt, make extra. Gingerbread House Royal Icing is best used the same day and doesn't

store well for next-day piping. If you need to pause while working, keep the icing covered with a damp cloth. It will stay workable for several hours without drying out.

**Day 3: Decorating/Party Day**—On the day you plan to decorate, you'll need a generous amount of icing for spreading on the rooftops and for filling decorating tubes. Plan on one batch of Gingerbread House Royal Icing per house for decorating day. For example, if you're prepping six houses, make six batches of icing the day of the party. We typically make three double batches and add them all to one large bowl. Keep the icing covered with a damp cloth to prevent it from drying out.

> *Tip:* Making a lot of houses? Stock up on powdered sugar; you'll go through more than you think! It's also a good idea to have extra egg whites and cream of tartar on hand to avoid mid-project runs to the store.

# Gingerbread House Royal Icing

*We've spent years perfecting this recipe, and it's our go-to for gingerbread houses of all shapes and sizes. It dries strong and sturdy, making it ideal for stabilizing walls, rooftops, and candy embellishments, yet pipes smoothly for small details and decorations. It's not the kind of icing you'll want to eat by the spoonful, but it's the secret to a gingerbread that is structurally sound!*

MAKES APPROXIMATELY 3 ½ CUPS

½ cup liquid egg whites (or 4 large egg whites)

½ teaspoon cream of tartar

5 cups powdered sugar (also called confectioners' sugar)

*Tip:* If you buy powdered sugar in 1-pound boxes, each 1-pound box equals roughly 3 cups.

*Gingerbread House Royal Icing for Cookies:* If you're using royal icing to pipe fine details on cookies, reduce the powdered sugar to 3 to 4 cups (instead of 5). This creates a slightly thinner (but still sturdy) icing that flows more easily through small piping tips.

In a large bowl, using a stand mixer fitted with the paddle attachment (or a hand mixer), beat the egg whites and cream of tartar on medium speed until frothy. Gradually add the powdered sugar, 1 cup at a time, beating well after each addition. Pause to scrape down the bowl. Continue beating for 5 full minutes or until the mixture is thick and fluffy and holds stiff peaks.

If the icing is too loose, add more powdered sugar, several tablespoons at a time, until it reaches a pipeable consistency. (Humidity can affect this, so adjust accordingly.) You're aiming for stiff peaks. When you drag a knife through the icing, it shouldn't run back together. This ensures the piped details hold their shape. If the icing becomes too thick to pipe, thin it with water just 1 tablespoon at a time.

Royal icing dries out quickly, so be sure to keep it covered with a damp cloth while you work. It's best used right away, but if it begins to firm up in the bowl, just beat it again for a minute or two to bring it back to a smooth, workable texture.

## FILLING THE PIPING BAG

Place a piping bag (fit with a piping tip) point-side down inside a tall glass or jar. Fold down the top of the bag over the rim of the glass and spoon icing into the bag. Unfold the top, twist to seal, and you're ready to decorate.

If you're piping extra-large, fluffy borders (like we do on our houses), allow extra drying time for the icing to fully harden.

# Mini Graham Cracker Houses Tutorial

*We also love making miniature graham cracker houses. At our tea party, we place one at each setting on a tiny cake stand. It's a simple detail that always delights. The girls love taking them home to their favorite doll or teddy bear, and they make the sweetest party favors. You can also group several together to create a charming little gingerbread village for your centerpiece, mantel, or windowsill.*

**1. Start with a 2 x 2-Inch Cardboard Box:** This forms the base of the mini house. There's no need to add a roof structure or triangular side supports out of cardboard like the larger version. You'll use graham cracker instead.

**2. Bottom (Optional):** You can hot glue a 2 x 2-inch graham cracker to the underside of the box for a finished look if you wish.

**3. Front and Back Pieces:** Take two full graham crackers (5 x 2¼ inches) from the box and trim just the top short edge of each piece into a triangle peak and glue them into place on opposite sides of the box to form the front and back of the house.

**4. Attach the Sides:** Use two 2 x 2-inch graham cracker squares and glue them to the remaining sides of the box. You may need to slightly trim the graham cracker square to fit these measurements.

**5. Add the Roof:** Carefully snap a whole graham cracker into two roof panel pieces (2½ inches each). No need to trim these pieces. Hot glue the two roof panels to the top edges of the sides to form a peaked roof.

**6. Flip and Pipe:** Just like the full-size version, flip the house upside down and place in a small bowl to hold it steady. Pipe Gingerbread House Royal Icing along all four edges of the bottom of the house. We use a small star piping tip, such as #21. *You can skip this step if you prefer the house to sit flat without the extra icing underneath.*

Let dry several hours or until hard to the touch, then flip upright and pipe sides and roof.

**7. Decorate:** Add a mini bow on top and use miniature candies like red hots, sprinkles, or gumdrops cut into small pieces.

CONDUCTOR
Michael
CONDUCTOR
Patrick
William

# *The* GINGERBREAD TRAIN PARTY

*All aboard the Gingerbread Express!*

Over the years, I've had hundreds of readers reach out asking how to re-create the pink-filled Gingerbread House Tea Party in a way that feels just as special for boys, as well as for parties that include both boys and girls. Gingerbread houses are for everyone, so while you can certainly adjust the color scheme of a gingerbread house party to blues, greens, or other wintry hues, this time I wanted to create something entirely its own.

Some of my dearest friends are boy moms, and I knew I wanted to celebrate them as well. While trains are certainly loved by girls too (we read *The Polar Express* each Christmas Eve at our house), a gingerbread train party felt like the perfect way to honor all the little gentlemen of Christmas.

In this chapter, you'll find everything you need to bring it to life, from candy-filled gingerbread train cars to a showstopping centerpiece train made entirely of gingerbread. Serve it all with gingerbread hot cocoa and the best gingerbread cookies you've ever tasted. Every detail is here to help you create the most magical Christmas train celebration.

Patrick

# Gingerbread Hot Cocoa

*This cozy cocoa tastes like classic hot chocolate with a hint of gingerbread spice. It's perfect for sipping at your gingerbread train party or curling up by the Christmas tree for a holiday movie night with family.*

SERVES 6 TO 8

¼ cup unsweetened cocoa powder

⅓ cup hot water

½ cup brown sugar

1 tablespoon unsulfured molasses

4 ½ cups milk (dairy or nondairy)

1 ½ cups heavy cream

2 teaspoons ground ginger

2 teaspoons ground cinnamon

¼ teaspoon ground nutmeg

Pinch of salt

1 teaspoon vanilla extract

## GARNISH ON TOP

Miniature marshmallows, ground cinnamon, and gingerbread cookies

In a small saucepan, whisk together the cocoa powder, hot water, brown sugar, and molasses until smooth and fully dissolved.

Add the milk and heavy cream and warm over medium heat, whisking occasionally, until the mixture is warmed through but not boiling.

Stir in the ginger, cinnamon, nutmeg, salt, and vanilla. Continue whisking gently until everything is well combined and fragrant.

Garnish with miniature marshmallows, a dash of cinnamon, and a gingerbread cookie too!

*Recipe Tip:* Cinnamon and peppermint sticks make great hot cocoa stirrers.

# Gingerbread Men Cookies

*If you've ever tried to nibble on a gingerbread house wall, this one's for you. This soft, spiced dough is made for eating, not building, and works beautifully with any cutout shape.*

MAKES 24 COOKIES

1 ½ sticks (¾ cup) unsalted butter

½ cup packed dark brown sugar

¼ cup granulated sugar

¾ cup unsulfured molasses

2 teaspoons vanilla extract

1 tablespoon heavy cream or whole milk

1 teaspoon salt

1 tablespoon ground cinnamon

2 teaspoons ground ginger

¼ teaspoon ground nutmeg

¼ teaspoon ground cloves

1 large egg, room temperature

3 ½ cups all-purpose flour

½ teaspoon baking soda

Gingerbread House Royal Icing for Cookies (page 41)

Melt the butter in a microwave-safe bowl or a medium saucepan over low heat. Remove from the heat and stir in the brown sugar, granulated sugar, molasses, vanilla, cream, salt, and spices. Whisk until smooth.

Transfer the mixture to a large mixing bowl and let it cool to lukewarm. Whisk in the egg.

In a separate bowl, whisk together the flour and baking soda. Gradually stir the dry ingredients into the wet mixture until a soft dough forms. You can add 1 to 2 tablespoons more flour if the dough feels *very* sticky. Dough will be tacky but should not stick to your finger when pressed.

Divide the dough in half, pat each portion into a disk, wrap tightly in plastic wrap, and refrigerate for at least 2 hours.

Preheat the oven to 350 degrees F.

Roll out the dough directly onto a sheet of parchment paper or a silicone baking mat to about ¼-inch thickness. Cut into shapes using cookie cutters, then gently peel away the excess dough. Transfer the entire piece of parchment paper to a baking sheet to avoid stretching the shapes with a spatula.

For the cleanest edges, chill the cutout shapes on the baking sheet for 5 to 10 minutes before baking.

For a soft and chewy texture, bake for 7 to 9 minutes, or until the edges are set and the centers look just firm. Let the cookies cool on the pan for a few minutes before transferring to a wire rack.

For crisper cookies, roll the dough slightly thinner and bake for 10 to 12 minutes.

Pipe royal icing on the gingerbread men to add details.

# Gingerbread Train Tutorial (Individual Trains)

*These gingerbread trains have become one of our favorite holiday touches. Lined up at each place setting for our littlest conductors, they never fail to bring smiles (and a bit of sugar-fueled excitement) to the table.*

Template pieces: Page 135

To begin, prepare one batch of the Gingerbread Construction Dough (page 76). One full batch is enough to make one complete train (one engine + one train car = one full train).

Use the gingerbread train template measurements in the back of the book to create your own template pieces out of card stock or poster board. Simply measure and cut each shape using the provided dimensions. Once made, your templates can be saved and reused over and over again.

Preheat the oven to 350 degrees F. Roll out the dough on a lightly floured silicone baking mat or sheet of parchment paper to about ¼ inch thick. Use the templates to cut out the following pieces:

### PIECES YOU'LL NEED

#### ENGINE

Engine Roof (1)

Engine Front (1)

Engine Sides (2)

Engine Back (1)

Engine Bottom (1)

Rounded Train Front (3)

Train Guard (1)

Wheels (4)

#### TRAIN CAR

Train Car Bottom (1)

Train Car Sides (2)

Train Car Front and Back (2)

Wheels (4)

Once you've cut out the pieces, lift the entire baking mat or sheet of parchment paper and place it directly onto a baking sheet. If you've taken your time or if the dough has softened, chill for 5 to 10 minutes before baking to help the shapes hold. If you're cutting and baking right away, you can skip this step. Reroll the

extra dough and continue until you have all the pieces made.

Bake the pieces until lightly golden and set. Depending on the size and shape, baking time will range from 8 to 12 minutes. Small pieces like the wheels will bake more quickly than the larger pieces. You can remove the smaller pieces early and return the tray to the oven to finish baking the rest. The pieces may feel slightly soft when they come out, but they will firm up as they cool. Once cooled, let them dry uncovered for several hours or overnight to ensure maximum sturdiness for assembly.

You can use either hot glue or royal icing for assembly, no judgment either way. Hot glue is ideal if you're short on time and want quick, sturdy results. If you'd prefer to keep the train fully edible, royal icing is the way to go. Just keep in mind that while technically edible, the assembled train will be quite hard once fully dried, so it's better to admire it and enjoy soft Gingerbread Men Cookies (page 50) on the side instead.

## ROYAL ICING AMOUNTS

Plan on one batch of Gingerbread House Royal Icing (page 41) for the assembly and borders of two full trains. For decorating on party day, plan on roughly one batch of icing for every two to three trains.

## ASSEMBLING THE TRAIN

Using the engine bottom as the base, attach the engine front, back, and two side panels on top of the bottom piece. Once those are in place, secure the roof piece. Hold or prop each section for a few minutes to help it set, then allow the icing or glue to dry completely. Finish the engine by attaching the four wheels with small

dabs of icing or glue. The rounded train front and train guard will be added later.

To assemble the train car, attach the two long side panels and the two shorter end pieces on top of the train car bottom to create a rectangular box. Add the four wheels to the sides once the base structure has set.

## FROSTING ON THE TRACKS (OPTIONAL)

For an added touch, flip the assembled engine and train car upside down and pipe a fluffy border of royal icing around the base to mimic snow. Let dry completely before flipping back. It adds an extra bit of drying time, but it's a charming detail if you have time. Otherwise, continue below with the next step.

Now you can begin adding our Gingerbread House Royal Icing to the train sides and using a small star tip (#32) to attach the rounded train front. Piping a swirl of icing between each rounded train front creates a layered, arched effect to the front of the engine. Once the rounded fronts are in place, add the train guard to the front, secured with a line of icing or glue at the base. Using a small round tip (such as #3), add charming details like wheel spokes, window embellishments, and bars on the train guard.

## STORAGE TIP

Once the gingerbread trains are fully assembled and dry, store them in a large plastic container with a lid to keep them protected until party time. Be sure the container is tall enough to avoid smudging any piped details.

On party day, set out each assembled gingerbread train with a bag of Gingerbread House Royal Icing and a variety of candies to let your little "conductors" decorate to their heart's content.

CONDUCTOR
Patrick

# Large Centerpiece Gingerbread Train Tutorial

*All aboard! This large gingerbread train makes a grand entrance down the center of the table, carrying cookies, candy, and plenty of delicious Christmas cargo.*

Template pieces: Page 136

Use the gingerbread train template measurements in the back of the book to create your own template pieces out of card stock or poster board. Simply measure and cut each shape using the listed dimensions. Once made, the templates can be saved and reused over and over.

Preheat the oven to 350 degrees F. Roll out a batch of the Gingerbread Construction Dough on a lightly floured silicone baking mat or sheet of parchment paper to about ¼ inch thick. Because of the size and detail of this larger train, you'll need multiple batches of gingerbread dough. The exact amount depends on how many train cars you plan to add.

Use the templates to cut out the following pieces:

- One batch will make the engine (including the four wheels).
- One batch will make the rounded front pieces (including stovepipe, wheels, and bottom).
- One batch will make two full train cars, wheels included.

### PIECES YOU'LL NEED

#### ENGINE

Engine Top (1)

Engine Front/Back (2)

Engine Sides (2)

Engine Bottom (1)

Wheels (4)

#### ROUNDED TRAIN FRONT

Curved Train Front (1)

Train Front Cap (1)

Train Front Bottom (1)

Train Guard (1)

Train Front Wheels (4)

Smokestack (1)

#### TRAIN CAR

Train Car Bottom (1)

Train Car Sides (2)

Train Car Front and Back (2)

Wheels (4)

Once you've cut out the large train pieces, lift the entire baking mat or sheet of parchment paper and place it directly onto a baking sheet. While one baking sheet is in the oven, reroll the excess dough out to continue making the template pieces. If some time has passed or if the dough has softened, chill for 5 to 10 minutes before baking to help the shapes hold. If you're cutting and baking right away, you can skip this step.

Bake the pieces until lightly golden and set. Depending on the size and shape, bake time will range from 10 to 14 minutes. Smaller pieces like the wheels will bake more quickly than the larger pieces. You can remove the smaller pieces early and return the tray to the oven to finish baking the rest. The pieces may feel slightly soft when they come out, but they will firm up as they cool. Once cooled, let them dry uncovered for several hours or overnight to ensure maximum sturdiness for assembly.

Once all the pieces are baked and cooled, you're ready to assemble the large train.

## LARGE TRAIN ASSEMBLY

### ENGINE

Start with the engine. As with the smaller trains, you can use either hot glue or royal icing for assembly.

Using the engine bottom as the base, attach the engine front, back, and two side panels on top. Once those are in place, secure the engine top piece. Hold or prop each section for a few minutes to help it set, then allow the icing or glue to dry completely. Finish the engine by attaching the four wheels with small dabs of icing or glue.

### ROUNDED FRONT

This is a more advanced gingerbread technique, but it creates such a charming effect, especially on train fronts, castle towers, and other rounded features. If you're up for the challenge, follow these steps carefully.

Rounded dough can be a bit finicky, but it's worth it for the final look. To make the curved front piece, cut the dough using the curved train front template. Place a 5½-inch aluminum food can (label removed, cleaned, and dried) directly on a silicone baking mat or a baking sheet lined with parchment paper. Gently lay the dough piece over the can to create the curved shape as shown in the picture.

Bake with the can in place, and allow the piece to cool completely on the can after baking. I like to leave the can inside permanently for support, but you could remove it once the gingerbread is fully cooled and firm; just be gentle if you choose to do so.

To make the smokestack, wrap a large metal piping tip (1M or similar) with a strip of gingerbread dough and place it upright on the baking sheet. Bake with the tip in place to help the dough hold its shape. Once cooled, you can leave the tip inside for support or gently remove it if preferred.

### TRAIN CARS

To assemble each train car, attach the two train car sides and the train car front and back pieces on top of the train car bottom to create a rectangular box. Add the four wheels to the sides once the base structure has set.

## FROSTING ON THE TRACKS (OPTIONAL)

For the same snowy effect as the individual trains, you can opt to frost the "tracks" of the larger train pieces. To do so, flip over the rounded train front bottom (before attaching the curved train front), assembled engine, and each train car, then pipe a fluffy border of royal icing along the base of each. Let dry completely (ideally overnight) before flipping them back over to continue assembly and decorating.

To finish the front of the train, attach the baked curved train front to the rounded train front bottom with royal icing or hot glue. Next, attach the train front cap to the front of the curved train front. Attach the smokestack to the top of the curved train front with royal icing or hot glue. Attach the four wheels to the train front as seen in the picture.

## DECORATING THE LARGE GINGERBREAD TRAIN

Use Gingerbread House Royal Icing (page 41) with a large star tip (such as 4B) to pipe borders around the engine, train car, and rounded train car front.

**Smokestack:** For the smokestack, border the bottom and top with Gingerbread House Royal Icing and a small star tip (such as #21 or #32). For a whimsical touch, stretch out a cotton ball and tuck it into the top to mimic a puff of steam.

**Train wheels:** Keep things classic with just piped icing, or embellish the wheels with peppermint candies for a festive pop of color.

**Train cars:** Fill the train cars with gumdrops and other candies, miniature gingerbread cookies, lollipops and more.

When ready to display, place the rounded train front, engine, and cars in the center of the tablescape.

> *Assembly Tip:* For easier handling, do not attach the rounded train front directly to the engine or link the train cars together. Keeping the pieces separate makes it much easier to lift and move them without risking cracks or breaks. Once everything is in place on the display, they'll still look beautifully connected.

Elizabeth

# *The* GINGERBREAD HOUSE DECORATING PARTY

*Sip, swirl, and decorate: Gingerbread isn't just for kids!*

Over the years of hosting gingerbread house tea parties for our children, the mothers and I often found ourselves saying the same thing: "We want a party too!" Why should the kids have all the fun? I've been decorating gingerbread houses since I could barely walk, yet it's so often treated as a childhood activity. I'm here to change that, because gingerbread houses are for everyone, from ages 1 to 101.

In this chapter, you'll find everything you need to re-create this magical Christmas gathering, from the signature cocktail and elegant hors d'oeuvres to a decadent dessert and the full step-by-step tutorial for a gingerbread house from scratch. Let this be your guide to hosting a holiday celebration for the adults that's every bit as beautiful as it is joy-filled.

So this year, gather your dearest friends during the Christmas season and set your table for a Gingerbread House Decorating Party. It's just as delightful for a girls' night as it is for a cozy couples' celebration. Serve gingerbread martinis garnished with tiny cookies, alongside an assortment of appetizers and small, festive bites.

Set the scene with elegance and a touch of festive flair: Fill crystal bowls with candies for decorating, tie long red velvet ribbons to the chandelier for an extra dose of glamour, line the table with glowing taper candles, and tuck candy canes into simple vases filled with red roses and winter berries.

And the main event: the gingerbread house! While graham cracker houses are a favorite, for this gathering, we opted for real gingerbread houses, complete with delicate windows and flickering votives tucked inside for a cozy, glowing charm. As with our children's parties, the houses are assembled in advance so guests can dive straight into decorating, sipping, and celebrating together.

# Ivy's Gingerbread Layer Cake

*Named for my younger daughter, this cake quickly became a family favorite after many rounds of recipe testing. Ivy was my most devoted (and enthusiastic) taste tester for this cake. Serve it as the grand finale at your Gingerbread House Decorating Party or as a sweet finish to Christmas Eve dinner. Decorate with an assortment of gingerbread house and tree-shaped gingerbread cookies and sugared rosemary sprigs for a snowy, storybook look. It's Ivy's favorite for a reason, and we have a feeling it might become yours too.*

MAKES 1 (2-LAYER, 8- OR 9-INCH) CAKE AND SERVES 12 TO 16

2 ¾ cups cake flour

2 teaspoons baking powder

1 teaspoon baking soda

½ teaspoon salt

2 teaspoons ground ginger

2 teaspoons ground cinnamon

½ teaspoon allspice

¼ teaspoon ground nutmeg

½ teaspoon ground cloves

¾ cup unsulfured molasses

¾ cup dark brown sugar

¼ cup granulated sugar

¾ cup plus 2 tablespoons vegetable oil

½ cup unsalted butter (1 stick), melted

2 large eggs, room temperature

1 large egg yolk, room temperature

2 teaspoons vanilla extract

1 cup buttermilk, room temperature

Preheat the oven to 350 degrees F. Grease and flour two 8- or 9-inch round cake pans, or line them with parchment paper for easy removal. Eight-inch pans will yield slightly taller layers, while 9-inch pans will yield wider, thinner layers. Both work well; just keep an eye on the bake time and test for doneness with a toothpick.

In a large bowl, whisk together the cake flour, baking powder, baking soda, salt, ginger, cinnamon, allspice, nutmeg, and cloves.

In a separate bowl, whisk together the molasses, dark brown sugar, granulated sugar, vegetable oil, and melted butter. Add the eggs, egg yolk, and vanilla, and whisk until smooth and well combined.

Gradually add the dry ingredients to the wet mixture, alternating with the buttermilk. Begin and end with the dry ingredients, mixing until just combined. Do not overmix.

Divide the batter evenly between the prepared pans and smooth the tops. Bake for 25 to 30 minutes or until a toothpick inserted into the center comes out clean.

Cool the cakes in the pans for 10 minutes, then turn the cakes out and transfer to a wire rack to cool completely before frosting and assembling.

*Continued*

## SUGAR AND SPICE FROSTING

MAKES ENOUGH FOR FROSTING 1 (8- OR 9-INCH) CAKE

8 ounces cream cheese, softened

½ cup unsalted butter, softened

4 cups powdered sugar

½ teaspoon ground ginger

1 teaspoon ground cinnamon

¼ teaspoon ground nutmeg

¼ teaspoon ground cloves

1 teaspoon vanilla extract

1 to 2 tablespoons heavy cream, as needed for consistency

In the bowl of a stand mixer fitted with the paddle attachment (or using a handheld electric mixer), beat the softened cream cheese and butter together on medium speed until smooth and fluffy, 3 to 4 minutes, making sure there are no lumps.

Gradually add the powdered sugar, 1 cup at a time, beating on low until incorporated. Once all the sugar is added, increase to medium speed and beat for another 2 to 3 minutes, until light and fluffy.

Add the ginger, cinnamon, nutmeg, cloves, and vanilla. Beat again until the spices are fully blended throughout.

If the frosting is too thick to spread, add heavy cream 1 tablespoon at a time until it reaches a spreadable consistency. If frosting is too thin, add more powdered sugar 1 tablespoon at a time.

Jessica

# Gingerbread Martini

*This Gingerbread Martini is rich, creamy, spiced, and perfect for sipping while decorating houses.*

MAKES 1 GINGERBREAD MARTINI

1 ½ ounces vodka

1 ounce Kahlúa

1 ounce heavy cream

1 ounce Gingerbread Syrup (page 131)

## GARNISH ON TOP

Ground nutmeg, cinnamon, and mini gingerbread cookie

In a cocktail shaker filled with ice, combine the vodka, Kahlúa, heavy cream, and gingerbread syrup. Shake vigorously until well chilled and frothy. Strain into a chilled coupe or martini glass.

For an extra festive touch, garnish with a mini gingerbread cookie on the rim and a light dusting of ground nutmeg or cinnamon.

*Make It a Batch:* Serving a crowd? Multiply the ingredients by the number of guests, then stir everything together in a large pitcher. Cover and refrigerate until ready to serve. Give it a good stir before pouring into chilled glasses.

# Spiced Pecan and Brie Puff Pastry Bites

*These little pastry bites have become one of my favorite holiday appetizers. They're flaky, buttery, and have the perfect mix of savory and sweet. I love making them at Christmastime when I want to serve something that feels a little fancy but is secretly so simple.*

MAKES 24 PASTRY BITES

1 sheet puff pastry, thawed

8 ounces Brie, cut into ½-inch cubes

1 egg, beaten

½ cup Spiced Gingerbread Pecans (page 121)

Fresh rosemary sprigs, for garnish

Honey, for drizzling, optional

Preheat the oven to 375 degrees F and grease a mini muffin pan.

Roll out the puff pastry on a lightly floured surface. Cut into 24 squares.

Press each square into the wells of the prepared pan, ensuring the edges come up around the sides. Place a cube of Brie into the center of each pastry square. Brush the edges of the puff pastry with the beaten egg for a golden finish.

Bake for 12 to 15 minutes, or until the puff pastry is puffed and golden and the Brie is melted. After baking, top each bite with a spiced pecan and a small sprig of fresh rosemary. If desired, drizzle with honey for an added touch of sweetness. Feeling spicy? Try drizzling them with Hot Honey (page 73) instead!

*Tip:* Assemble the pastry bites in advance to save time on party day! Prior to adding the egg wash, wrap the mini muffin tray tightly with plastic wrap or aluminum foil and refrigerate for up to 2 days. Remove from refrigerator, brush with egg wash, bake, and top with spiced pecans, rosemary, and honey.

# Rosemary and Parmesan Shortbread with Whipped Goat Cheese

*Use your favorite holiday cookie cutters for appetizers too. These savory rosemary and Parmesan shortbread crackers are a delicious addition to any Christmas spread.*

MAKES 20 TO 24 CRACKERS

## SHORTBREAD

¾ cup (1½ sticks) unsalted butter, softened

1½ cups all-purpose flour

1 cup finely grated Parmesan cheese

2 tablespoons finely chopped fresh rosemary, plus more for garnish

1 teaspoon fresh orange zest, optional

¼ teaspoon salt

1 teaspoon freshly ground black pepper

Preheat oven to 325 degrees F and line a baking sheet with parchment paper.

In a food processor, add the softened butter, the flour, Parmesan, rosemary, orange zest (if using), salt, and black pepper. Process until the dough comes together into a soft ball.

On a lightly floured surface, roll out the dough to about ¼ inch thick. Sprinkle with a bit of fresh rosemary, to garnish, then top with a sheet of wax paper. Gently roll over the wax paper with a rolling pin to press the rosemary into the dough. Lift off the wax paper, press a tree-shaped cookie cutter into the shortbread, and carefully peel away the excess dough.

Bake for 12 to 15 minutes, or until the edges are lightly golden. Let cool completely on a wire rack. Handle carefully to avoid crumbling. Serve with Whipped Goat Cheese.

## WHIPPED GOAT CHEESE

MAKES 1 CUP WHIPPED GOAT CHEESE

4 ounces soft goat cheese

4 ounces cream cheese, softened

2 tablespoons heavy cream

1 teaspoon finely chopped fresh rosemary

Salt and freshly ground black pepper

In a food processor or stand mixer, combine the goat cheese, cream cheese, heavy cream, and rosemary. Whip until smooth and creamy. Season with salt and pepper to taste. Transfer to a serving bowl and keep refrigerated until ready to serve. Remove at least 20 minutes before serving to allow it to soften.

*Optional Garnishes:* Drizzle with Hot Honey (see recipe on opposite page) or top with pomegranate arils.

### HOT HONEY

1 cup honey

2 to 3 teaspoons red pepper flakes (adjust to your spice preference)

2 teaspoons apple cider vinegar

In a small saucepan, heat the honey and red pepper flakes over medium heat just until it begins to boil. Immediately remove from the heat and stir in the apple cider vinegar. Strain to remove the pepper flakes and let cool.

Simmer + Spice
Simmer + Spice
Simmer + Spice

# Christmas Simmer Pot Favor Bags

*These simmer pot favor bags are one of my favorite gifts to give during the holidays. They're simple, thoughtful, and quick to make. Tucked into clear cone bags and tied with velvet ribbon and a little "Simmer and Spice" tag, they're festive and fragrant before they even hit the stovetop. Set out on a silver tray, they double as beautiful party decor and cozy take-home favor.*

## WHAT TO INCLUDE IN EACH SIMMER POT FAVOR BAG

1 whole orange

2 or 3 cinnamon sticks

A generous sprinkle of whole cloves

A small handful of star anise

⅓ cup fresh cranberries

2 or 3 fresh rosemary sprigs

Pack all the ingredients into a clear cellophane cone bag and tie with a velvet ribbon and tag. For a little extra flair, tuck a dried orange slice on top. Add a small tag with instructions on the back or place a small framed sign beside the favor bags so guests know how to use them. Here's what I like to include:

Slice the orange and combine all ingredients in a saucepan with 3 to 4 cups of water. Simmer on low, adding more water as needed. It's beginning to smell a lot like Christmas!

## DRIED ORANGE SLICES

These charming dried orange slices are a holiday favorite around here. I use them in all sorts of ways, such as tying them onto simmer pot favor bags, tucking them into Christmas Citrus Topiary (page 84), string them into garlands for the tree, and more.

To make them, carefully slice an orange into thin rounds using a sharp knife or mandoline. Discard the ends. Line a baking sheet with parchment paper. Dip both sides of each orange slice in a shallow bowl of powdered sugar and place them on the lined sheet.

Bake at 200 degrees F for 2 hours, or until the slices are dried and lightly golden. Remove from the oven and let cool completely. Store in an airtight container.

# Gingerbread Construction Dough

*This is the gingerbread dough that's just right for building real gingerbread houses. It's simple to make, comes together like a dream, and won't puff or spread too much in the oven, so the pieces hold their shape beautifully. Best of all, it doesn't require any chilling if you're baking it right away. We absolutely love this dough for houses, gingerbread ornaments, gingerbread sleighs, and more.*

MAKES ENOUGH DOUGH TO ROLL INTO A ROUGHLY 11 X 17-INCH RECTANGLE. ONE BATCH WILL MAKE ONE INDIVIDUAL TRAIN (PAGE 53) OR ONE COTTAGE-SIZE GINGERBREAD HOUSE (PAGE 90).

½ cup (1 stick) butter, softened

½ cup granulated sugar

½ cup unsulfured molasses

1 large egg, room temperature

3 cups all-purpose flour

1 teaspoon ground ginger

1 teaspoon ground cinnamon

1 teaspoon ground cloves

*Note:* While this gingerbread dough is technically edible, it's not the best for eating, so we recommend snacking on the Gingerbread Men Cookies (page 50) instead.

In the bowl of a stand mixer fitted with the paddle attachment, cream the butter and sugar together for about 2 minutes, until light and fluffy. Add the molasses and egg and mix again for about 30 seconds, until just combined. Pause to scrape down the sides of the bowl as needed to make sure everything is evenly mixed.

Slowly add the flour, ginger, cinnamon, and cloves. Mix on low speed until a soft, workable dough forms. The dough may feel slightly tacky to the touch, but if it's very sticky, add a tablespoon of flour at a time.

Sprinkle your hands with a dusting of flour and remove the dough from the bowl (I love to use a bowl scraper to help). Lightly dust the work surface or a silicone mat with flour. Form the dough ball into a rectangular shape. Dust a rolling pin with flour and roll out the dough into a large rectangle, trying to keep the same thickness. Periodically sprinkle additional flour as needed if sticky. I keep a small bowl of flour by my work surface.

When ready to cut, use cookie cutters or lay the templates on top of the rolled dough and carefully cut out with a sharp knife. If edges are sticky, dip the tip of the knife in flour as you cut.

Peel away the excess dough and transfer the silicone mat to a baking sheet. This prevents you from having to scoop up the cutout pieces with a spatula, which often affects the shape.

Gather and reroll excess dough and trimming scraps to cut additional pieces. Just be careful not to overwork the dough, because too much handling can make it drier and less smooth than the original batch.

To save leftover dough, roll it into a ball and cover tightly with plastic wrap. Refrigerate for up to 3 days.

Bake at 350 degrees F. Bake time will depend on the size and thickness of the pieces. I typically bake small pieces for 8 to 10 minutes and larger ones for 12 to 15 minutes. The pieces may feel slightly soft when they come out of the oven, but they will firm up as they cool. Keep a close eye as they bake. It's better to slightly overbake than underbake to ensure the pieces are sturdy enough for building. If you find that the pieces are still soft after cooling, you can return them to the oven to bake for another few minutes.

Allow pieces to dry out, uncovered, in a cool, dry area.

# Classic Gingerbread House Tutorial

*There's nothing more timeless than a classic gingerbread house. This version uses sturdy, simple shapes that make it easy to build and endlessly fun to decorate. Add lattice-trimmed "glass" windows for an extra magical touch.*

## WHAT YOU'LL NEED

Gingerbread Construction Dough (page 76)

Gingerbread House Royal Icing (page 41)

Classic Gingerbread House template pieces (page 134)

Gelatin sheets or hard candies for windows, optional

Piping bags and piping tips

## TEMPLATE PIECES (CUT FROM DOUGH)

2 front/back panels

2 wall panels

2 roof panels

1 bottom panel, optional

1 door piece (for added dimension), optional

## MEASUREMENT NOTES

To make one full-size gingerbread house using the provided template measurements, you'll need:

- **2 batches** of Gingerbread Construction Dough (with a little extra left over)
- **1 batch** of Gingerbread House Royal Icing for assembling the house (acting as the "glue") or hot glue
- **1 additional batch** of Gingerbread House Royal Icing for decorating to be used for piping fluffy borders, spreading on the roof, and adding all the finishing details

## INSTRUCTIONS

**1. Create the Templates:** Using the provided measurements (page 134), draw each house piece onto poster board or card stock and cut them out to use as sturdy, reusable templates.

**2. Cut the Dough:** Roll out the construction dough and cut out using the templates.

*Note:* The front and back of the house are cut from the same template piece. You'll cut it twice. The same applies to the sides and roof panels.

Use a small knife to carefully cut out windows from all pieces before baking. Windows are optional, so you can leave the pieces solid if you prefer.

**3. Bake Template Pieces:** Bake all pieces according to the dough recipe. Let them cool completely on a flat surface to prevent any warping or bending.

**4. Window Designs (Optional)**

**"Glass" Windows:** Cut gelatin sheets to fit behind each window opening, leaving a small border. You can leave them plain or pipe lattice or decorative trim directly onto the gelatin sheets before attaching. Flip each wall panel over and use royal icing to adhere the gelatin sheets to the back of the window openings.

**Stained-Glass Windows:** For colorful stained-glass windows, sprinkle crushed hard candies (like Jolly Ranchers or Life Savers) into the window cutouts with 3 to 4 minutes left in the bake time of the gingerbread dough. The candy will melt and spread into a smooth, translucent finish. Let the pieces cool completely on the tray before removing.

**5. Assemble the House:** Start by attaching the front and back panels around the bottom piece, if using. Next, add the side panels. Pipe along the edges, gently press the pieces together, and hold until secure. Add additional royal icing in the interior corner seams for extra reinforcement. Attach the door piece to the front of the house for a 3D effect. Let the structure dry at least several hours before adding the roof panels.

During this time, cover the bowl of remaining royal icing with a damp towel to prevent it from drying out. Next, attach the roof panels with remaining icing (stir well to resoften). Hold the roof panels in place for a few minutes until set, using cans or other household items to help support the roof as it dries.

If small gaps remain after assembly, don't worry; the royal icing borders will hide them all! We recommend allowing the house to dry overnight before decorating.

**6. Add Icing Borders and Decorate:** Once assembled, use the second batch of royal icing to decorate the gingerbread house. We love adding our signature fluffy borders piped with a large star tip (4B or 1M) to the edges. Add candies, gumdrops, peppermints, and whatever whimsical touches you love most. Add a jingle bell doorknob or your favorite candy.

**Add Glow:** The bottom piece has a circle opening in the center to allow for an LED tea light to be tucked inside to softly illuminate the windows from within. You can also add a string of fairy lights.

**Pipe Icicles:** To create a classic icicle effect, use a small round piping tip and slightly thinned royal icing. Pipe a dot just under the roofline, then quickly pull down to form an icicle shape. If the icing is too stiff, add a touch of water or thicken it with sifted powdered sugar to reach the right consistency (smooth enough to flow, but thick enough to hold its shape).

# ENTERTAINING *at* CHRISTMAS *with* GINGERBREAD

*Sometimes the gingerbread doesn't land on the cookie tray;*
*it's tied to a napkin, tucked into a snow globe,*
*or nestled at every seat as a little holiday surprise.*

# Christmas Eve Celebration

*O come all ye faithful neighbors! Whether it's a neighborhood drop-in or your family's Christmas Eve tradition, nothing sets the tone like a red tablecloth and the sparkle of silver. Create a gorgeous citrus topiary centerpiece brimming with oranges, limes, apples, cloves, and more. Gingerbread houses made during the season come to life displayed on cake stands. Add chilled champagne, a big bowl of Christmas Party Fruit Tea (page 31), and sweet treats like Gingerbread Cheesecake Trifle (page 86) and you've got yourself a table full of holiday cheer and memories in the making.*

## WHAT YOU'LL NEED TO MAKE A CHRISTMAS CITRUS TOPIARY

1 large cake stand

1 small cake stand

1 Styrofoam tree shape (about 8 inches)

1 box of toothpicks

Assorted citrus fruits (clementines, oranges, satsumas, limes)

A few small apples, apricots, or nectarines

Whole cloves

Fresh greenery (magnolia leaves, ivy, cedar sprigs)

Small white flowers, spray roses, or seasonal blooms

Red ribbon, for trimming the top

Dried orange slices, miniature gingerbread cookies or sugared cranberries, optional

Place the small cake stand on top of the larger one, then set the Styrofoam cone on top of the small stand to elevate the arrangement. Starting at the bottom of the cone, use toothpicks to secure the citrus and other fruits, mixing colors and sizes as you go. Press whole cloves into a few of the fruits. Fill in any gaps with greenery and flowers. Top with a red ribbon and embellish with optional touches like dried oranges or gingerbread cookies.

*Sizing Tip:* If you don't have two cake stand sizes, no problem! Just use one large cake stand and opt for a slightly taller Styrofoam cone (10 to 12 inches) to create the same effect.

# Gingerbread Cheesecake Trifle

*An elegant dessert served in your favorite stemmed glassware is the perfect Christmas Eve dessert. Make it extra special by topping with a Petite Gingerbread House (page 98).*

MAKES 8 TO 10 TRIFLES

## GINGERBREAD CAKE

½ cup unsalted butter, melted

½ cup dark brown sugar

½ cup unsulfured molasses

1 large egg

1 cup buttermilk (or 1 cup milk and 1 tablespoon lemon juice)

1½ cups all-purpose flour

1 teaspoon baking soda

1½ teaspoons ground ginger

1 teaspoon ground cinnamon

¼ teaspoon ground cloves

¼ teaspoon ground nutmeg

¼ teaspoon salt

Preheat the oven to 350 degrees F. Grease and line a 9 x 13-inch baking pan with parchment paper.

In a large bowl, whisk together the melted butter, brown sugar, molasses, and egg. Stir in the buttermilk until smooth.

Add the flour, baking soda, spices, and salt. Stir until just combined.

Pour into the prepared pan and bake for 24 to 28 minutes, or until a toothpick comes out clean. Ovens vary, so watch carefully to prevent overbaking.

Cool completely, then cut into small cubes.

## WHIPPED CHEESECAKE LAYER

12 ounces (1½ blocks) cream cheese, softened

2½ to 3 cups powdered sugar

2 teaspoons vanilla extract

3 to 4 tablespoons milk or heavy cream

Beat the cream cheese, powdered sugar, and vanilla until smooth. Add milk, 1 tablespoon at a time, until the mixture is soft and creamy (spoonable, like thick mousse).

## ADDITIONAL TOPPING

½ cup store-bought caramel sauce

## GARNISH ON TOP

Crushed gingersnaps, sugared cranberries, sugared rosemary sprigs, or a Petite Gingerbread House (page 98)

In each stemmed glass, layer cubed gingerbread cake, a spoonful of cheesecake filling, and a drizzle of caramel sauce. Repeat the layers until each glass is full, ending with a drizzle of caramel. Refrigerate for at least 1 hour before serving.

Garnish just before serving with crushed cookies, a final drizzle of caramel, and a petite gingerbread house on top. These trifles can be made up to 1 day in advance, but garnish just before serving to keep toppings crisp and fresh.

# Gingerbread in the Garden

*Living in Charleston means we occasionally get the gift of mild December days, perfect for bringing the festivities to the garden. If your climate allows, setting a Christmas table outside is a festive way to celebrate the season.*

For this gathering, we layered a botanical holiday tablecloth with bamboo chairs and draped cozy red pashminas to the backs for staying warm. Each place was set with a handmade gingerbread cottage. With red roses, berries, and fresh greenery as the centerpiece, it's proof that gingerbread doesn't have to stay in the kitchen.

For the youngest guests, we set a miniature tea table in the garden with silver cups, tiny treats, and their very own gingerbread house. It made the celebration feel extra special and just their size.

# Gingerbread Cottage House Tutorial

*Smaller than the classic, this gingerbread cottage is one of our favorite sizes. We love to add these to place settings, display them on mantels, and give them as gifts. If you want to make real gingerbread houses with a group, for instance as part of a school classroom celebration, this is a great size to make.*

## WHAT YOU'LL NEED

Gingerbread Construction Dough (page 76)

Gingerbread House Royal Icing (page 41)

Gingerbread Cottage template pieces (page 137)

Piping bags and piping tips

## TEMPLATE PIECES (CUT FROM DOUGH)

2 front/back panels

2 side panels

2 roof panels

1 bottom panel (for added stability), optional

## MEASUREMENT NOTES

To make one full-size gingerbread cottage using the provided template measurements, you'll need:

- **1 batch** of Gingerbread Construction Dough
- **1 batch** of Gingerbread House Royal Icing for assembling the house (acting as the "glue") or hot glue
- **1 additional batch** of Gingerbread House Royal Icing for decorating. This will be used for piping fluffy borders, spreading on the roof, and adding all the finishing details.

## INSTRUCTIONS

**1. Create the Templates:** Using the provided measurements (page 137), draw each house piece onto poster board or card stock and cut them out to use as sturdy, reusable templates.

**2. Cut the Dough:** Roll out the construction dough and use the templates to cut the pieces.

> *Note:* The front and back of the house are cut from the same template piece. You'll cut it twice. The same applies to the sides and roof panels.

**3. Bake Template Pieces:** Bake all pieces according to the dough recipe. Let them cool completely on a flat surface to prevent any warping or bending.

**4. Assemble the House:** Start by attaching a front panel to the bottom panel with royal icing. Continue with the back panel and sides, piping along the edges of each piece. Gently press the pieces together and hold until secure. Add additional royal icing along the interior corner seams for extra reinforcement. Let the structure set up for several hours.

During this time, cover the bowl of remaining royal icing with a damp towel to prevent it from drying out. Next, attach the roof panels with remaining icing (stir well to resoften). Hold the roof panels in place for a few minutes until set, using cans or other household items to help support the roof as it dries.

If small gaps remain after assembly, don't worry; the royal icing borders will hide them all! We recommend allowing the house to dry overnight before decorating.

**5. Add Icing Borders and Decorate:** You will need a second batch of Gingerbread House Royal Icing to decorate the gingerbread house. On this size gingerbread house, we use a star tip (#32) for our signature fluffy icing borders. Add candies, gumdrops, peppermints, and whatever whimsical touches you love most.

# Icy Winter Holiday Tablescape with Mini House Snow Globes

*Step into an icy wonderland and set your holiday table with a magical snow globe scene featuring a Petite Gingerbread House waiting at each place setting. Add the soft glow of crystal votives, layers of blue-and-white china on a soft blue linen, and glass trees and reindeer to create the ultimate sparkling frosted tablescape.*

## RE-CREATE THE SNOW GLOBES

To make your own gingerbread house snow globes, follow the instructions for the Petite Gingerbread House on page 98. Once decorated, dust each house with powdered sugar for a "freshly fallen snow" effect. Tuck in a few sprigs of sugared rosemary to resemble icy trees on either side of the petite houses.

Set each one on a small plate or coaster sprinkled with coarse sparkling sugar and top with a glass cloche or miniature dome.

*Tip:* Use a dot of royal icing to help the trees stand up straight. Finish with a red velvet ribbon tied on top of the cloche.

Setting a whimsical scene like this at each place setting is a beautiful way to make your guests feel special, and it doubles as a take-home favor. These little snow globe houses can be packaged up in cellophane bags after dinner or tied with a name tag to double as a place card. Whether you're hosting a formal dinner or a casual holiday brunch with family, this is a simple idea that turns the table into something truly memorable.

## CENTERPIECE SNOW GLOBE

Turn the tiny snow globe idea into a full centerpiece by arranging several gingerbread houses under a domed glass cake stand. Add a dusting of "snow" (powdered sugar or faux snow) and tuck in a strand of fairy lights for a magical glow.

# Pretty-in-Pink Christmas Tablescape

*Think outside the box for more whimsical ways to incorporate gingerbread into your tablescapes. We love these miniature needlepoint stockings from Bauble Stockings made especially to match our annual Gingerbread House Tea Party. They are delightful set at each place setting and filled with a small gift, flowers, or candy. We also love tying them onto the back of the chairs with a big red bow at our tea party.*

# A Classic Christmas Tablescape

*When entertaining family and friends that we love, it is the little things that mean the most. These gingerbread house cookie place cards are as sweet in sentiment as they are in flavor.*

## GINGERBREAD HOUSE PLACE CARDS

Using the dough for Gingerbread Men Cookies (page 50), simply cut out house-shaped cookies, then use a straw to make a small hole near the top of each one before baking.

Once cooled, pipe guests' names with royal icing and allow them to dry completely. Thread a velvet ribbon through the top and tie each cookie around a neatly folded napkin.

Not only does this add a festive, handmade touch to each place setting, but it also doubles as a sweet takeaway. Make an extra for Santa and you'll be sure to land on the nice list.

We paired them with classic Christmas Spode china, a beloved pattern passed down through generations and a staple on many Southern holiday tables. First introduced in 1938, the Spode Christmas Tree has become a cherished heirloom in countless families. These personalized gingerbread house cookies add just the right touch of sweetness and whimsy to a table full of tradition. And, between us, I have a feeling Mrs. Claus sets her table with Christmas Spode too.

## FESTIVE TWISTS

**Try different shapes:** Use stars, trees, or stockings instead of house-shaped cookies for a fun twist.

**Play with color:** Tint the royal icing with soft pastels or bold reds and greens to match the tablescape.

**Add sparkle:** A touch of edible glitter or coarse sugar gives each cookie a magical shimmer.

**Swap the ribbon:** Use baker's twine, gold thread, or plaid ribbon to match your holiday style.

**Make ahead:** Bake and decorate the cookies in advance and store in an airtight container until you're ready to set the table.

# CRAFTING *with* GINGERBREAD

*Welcome to the Gingerbread Workshop!*

While gingerbread is delicious to eat, some of the most charming ways to enjoy it are in special Christmas crafts. In this chapter you'll find different ways of using gingerbread and candies to create centerpieces, gifts, decorations, and more.

# Petite Gingerbread House

*As shown on page 96. These extra tiny gingerbread houses are a personal favorite. We love to use them as mug toppers and tiny gifts, and we also tuck them inside snow globes.*

## WHAT YOU'LL NEED

Petite Gingerbread House template pieces (page 138)

Poster board or card stock

Gingerbread Construction Dough (page 76)

Gingerbread House Royal Icing (page 41)

Small piping bags and fine piping tips

Small candies, optional

## INSTRUCTIONS

**1. Create the Templates:** Use the provided petite house templates (page 138) to create and cut out the pieces from poster board or card stock. Each house requires six pieces: front, back, two sides, and two roof panels.

**2. Cut and Bake:** Roll out the construction dough and cut out each house piece using the templates. Because these are small, reduce the baking time, typically 7 to 8 minutes, but keep a close eye as ovens vary. Let pieces cool completely before assembling.

**3. Assemble the House:** Fill a small piping bag with royal icing and snip the tip (or use a small round piping tip). Pipe along the seams to attach the front, back, and side walls first. Then attach the roof pieces. Allow the icing to set completely before decorating. If you prefer, you can assemble with hot glue.

**4. Decorate:** Pipe fluffy borders along the roof and edges and, if you want to, add tiny candies for extra charm.

# Gingerbread Ornaments

*These classic ornaments are simple to make and bring a handmade, cozy touch to your holiday decor. They're perfect for hanging on trees, stringing into garlands, and using as gift toppers. The best part? They can be reused every year.*

## INSTRUCTIONS

**1. Make the Dough:** Prepare one batch of Gingerbread Construction Dough (page 76). This recipe bakes up firm and durable, ideal for long-lasting ornaments (for decorating only, not for eating).

**2. Roll and Cut:** Roll the dough out on a lightly floured surface and use your favorite holiday cookie cutters to cut out shapes. Try stars, trees, angels, gingerbread men, or even alphabet letters to spell names or festive words.

**3. Punch Holes:** Before baking, use a straw to gently punch a hole near the top of each ornament. This is where the ribbon will go. Be sure it's far enough from the edge to prevent breaking.

**4. Bake and Cool:** Bake according to the dough recipe instructions. Let the ornaments cool completely before handling.

**5. Decorate (Optional):** Leave them plain for a simple look or pipe on royal icing designs for extra charm. Let icing dry completely if decorating.

**6. String and Hang:** Thread ribbon, baker's twine, or metallic cord through the holes and tie securely. Hang on your tree, add to wreaths, or use as festive gift toppers.

**7. Store for Next Year:** If kept dry and stored in an airtight container, these ornaments can be reused for many years to come.

### *Try This: Gingerbread Jewelry*

Turn leftover dough into something extra sweet! Use mini cookie cutters to make tiny shapes, and don't forget to poke a hole before baking. Once cooled, string them together with ribbon or baker's twine to create charming bracelets and necklaces.

# Gingerbread Cookie Wreath

*This gingerbread cookie wreath is fun to make. Either hang it on your front door to greet guests or lay it flat on the table and fill the center with candles, greenery sprigs, or flowers for a showstopping centerpiece.*

## WHAT YOU'LL NEED

Wood wreath ring (found at most craft stores)

Assortment of Christmas cookie cutters (we used snowflakes)

1 to 2 batches of Construction Grade Gingerbread Dough

Gingerbread House Royal Icing (page 41) for decorating, optional

Strong hot glue (such as Gorilla Hot Glue Sticks)

Ribbon for hanging

## ASSEMBLY TIPS

**1. Prepare the Base:** You can wrap the wood ring in ribbon, but it's not necessary if you plan to fully cover it with cookies.

**2. Plan for Hanging:** Before attaching cookies, loop ribbon around the top for easy hanging, or attach a metal hanger to the back.

**3. Bake the Cookies:** Choose a mix of large and small cookie cutters. Bigger cookies form the base; smaller ones are perfect for layering and filling in gaps.

**4. Decorate:** Once cookies are baked and cooled, add royal icing details for a festive finish, if desired.

**5. Build the Wreath:** Start by gluing the larger cookies directly to the wreath base. Layer smaller cookies on top and around the edges for depth and dimension.

**6. Handle with Care:** Once assembled, the wreath will be sturdy but still delicate. Move and hang it gently.

These cookie wreaths are a joy to make and bring festive cheer to any corner of your home.

# Gingerbread Sleigh

*My mother has been making these little gingerbread sleighs for decades. They've graced our holiday tables, made magazine appearances, and become a favorite to make every year.*

## WHAT YOU'LL NEED

Sleigh template pieces (page 138)

Poster board or card stock

Gingerbread Construction Dough (page 76)

Gingerbread House Royal Icing (page 41)

Hot glue for quicker assembly, optional

Candy canes for sleigh runners

Assorted candies for decorating and filling

## INSTRUCTIONS

**1. Prepare the Templates:** Using the sleigh templates (large or small) as a guide, use a ruler to re-create the shapes on poster board or card stock and cut them out. You'll need five pieces per sleigh: two sides, a bottom, a front end, and a back end.

**2. Cut and Bake the Gingerbread:** Roll out the construction dough and use the templates to cut out the sleigh pieces. Bake according to the recipe instructions and allow them to cool completely before assembling.

**3. Assemble the Sleigh Base:** Using royal icing or hot glue, attach the side panels and end pieces (front and back) to the sleigh's bottom. If using royal icing, allow the sleigh to dry overnight to ensure it's fully set and sturdy before continuing.

**4. Decorate the Sleigh:** Once the sleigh is assembled and set, pipe decorative borders and designs using royal icing. We use a small star tip (#21). Let the icing dry completely, at least 4 hours, or preferably overnight.

**5. Attach the Runners:** Using hot glue (or royal icing with props for support), carefully attach two candy canes to the bottom of the sleigh to act as runners. For larger sleighs, use 7-inch candy canes; for smaller sleighs, 5½-inch candy canes work well.

> *Note:* In humid climates, candy canes can become sticky and fragile. Leaving them in their clear plastic wrapping helps preserve their structure and shine.

**6. Finish and Fill:** Once the sleigh is complete, fill it with mini candies, cookies, or even a tiny gift. Add a bow on the back for a finishing touch.

# Candy Trees

*While there's technically no gingerbread involved, these whimsical candy trees fit right in among the gumdrop lanes and peppermint paths of a gingerbread village. Imagine them lining the walkway to a storybook candy cottage. My daughters love decorating them with neighbors at Christmas. The kids love choosing their candies, designing their trees, picking their ribbon for bows, and proudly carrying them home to display.*

## WHAT YOU'LL NEED

Small flowerpot (clay or ceramic)

Styrofoam to fit snugly inside the pot for anchoring tree trunk

Acrylic candy canes (with curved tops trimmed off) or wooden dowels, painted festive colors

Tree-shaped Styrofoam form (we recommend 5- to 8-inch sizes)

Gingerbread House Royal Icing (page 41)

Assorted candies (gumdrops, peppermints, jelly beans, etc.)

Ribbon (large bow for the top and optional mini bows for decorating)

Moss for covering base, optional

## INSTRUCTIONS

**1. Prep the Pot:** Paint the flowerpot in a festive color if desired. Insert a block of Styrofoam into the pot so it fits snugly. This will anchor the tree trunk.

**2. Create the Tree Trunk:** Use a straight acrylic candy cane (cut to size) or a painted wooden dowel. Insert it firmly into the Styrofoam base, all the way to the bottom so it stands upright.

**3. Attach the Tree Form:** Push the flat end of the tree-shaped Styrofoam form down onto the top of the candy cane or dowel. Make sure it is pressed in far enough to be stable (at least a few inches).

**4. Decorate the Tree:** Spread royal icing over the tree using an offset spatula or the back of a spoon. Press candies into the icing to decorate. If you'd like to add piped details, use a piping bag with a fluted tip to create starbursts, ruffles, or garlands.

**5. Finishing Touches:** Top each tree with a big ribbon bow, and add smaller ones throughout if you'd like. Add moss, if using, around the base of the pot, or pipe royal icing and decorate with more candies.

*Hostess Tip:* If you're hosting a candy tree decorating party, consider pre-icing the Styrofoam trees about 30 minutes to an hour before guests arrive. This gives younger children a head start, and they can dive right into the decorating fun without waiting on the icing step. Older kids may prefer to add the icing themselves. Either way, we always set out extra piping bags filled with icing for securing larger candies and adding extra sweet details.

*Tree Size Tip:* We recommend using 5- to 8-inch Styrofoam tree forms. Anything larger can become unstable, especially once decorated, since sugar is surprisingly heavy. If you're set on creating a larger tree, you will need to anchor it in quick-set concrete rather than Styrofoam to give the base extra stability.

# Gingerbread Spice Tree

*These charming spice trees bring the scent of Christmas wherever they go. Instead of candy, they're decorated with warm holiday spices and miniature gingerbread cookies. Perfect as a hostess gift or kitchen windowsill accent, they're as lovely to give as they are to keep.*

## WHAT YOU'LL NEED

Small flowerpot (clay or ceramic)

Styrofoam to fit snugly inside the pot

Tree-shaped Styrofoam form (we recommend 5- to 8-inch sizes)

Elmer's glue

Ground ginger, cinnamon, cloves, and nutmeg, for coating

Long cinnamon sticks (or wooden dowels) for trunks

Star anise pods and whole cloves, for embellishing

Mini gingerbread cookies (stars or other small shapes made from construction-grade dough)

Moss, to cover the base; optional but recommended

Velvet ribbon (for a bow on top) spread

## INSTRUCTIONS

1. **Prep the Pot:** Paint the pot if desired, then insert a snug piece of Styrofoam inside to hold the tree trunk.

2. **Season the Tree Form:** Before assembling, coat the Styrofoam tree with Elmer's glue using a foam brush or your fingers (these trees are decorative, not edible). While the glue is still wet, gently roll the tree in a shallow plate of ground gingerbread spices until fully coated. Let dry completely before moving on.

3. **Assemble the Tree:** Insert a long cinnamon stick (or painted dowel) into the Styrofoam base to serve as the trunk. Press the dried, spice-coated tree form onto the top of the cinnamon stick, pushing it in a few inches to keep it stable.

4. **Decorate:** Use hot glue to attach decorative elements like star anise pods, whole cloves, and mini gingerbread cookies.

5. **Finishing Touch:** Add moss, if using, around the top of the pot to cover the base and add charm. Top the tree with a velvet bow.

# Gingerbread Playdough Recipe

*This soft, spiced dough smells just like the holidays and is perfect for little hands. Whether you're shaping pretend cookies or giving jars as gifts, it's a fun and festive activity the whole family will love.*

*This playdough is for play only and not intended for eating, even though it's made with food-safe ingredients.*

MAKES ABOUT 4 CUPS OF PLAYDOUGH

## WHAT YOU'LL NEED

2 cups all-purpose flour

¾ cup salt

4 teaspoons cream of tartar

2 tablespoons ground ginger

5 tablespoons ground cinnamon

1 teaspoon ground cloves

2 cups lukewarm water

3 tablespoons vegetable oil or coconut oil

2 tablespoons vanilla extract for extra fragrance, optional

2 tablespoons glycerin for added stretch and shine, optional

## INSTRUCTIONS

**1. Mix the Dry Ingredients:** In a large heat-safe pot, whisk together the flour, salt, cream of tartar, ginger, cinnamon, and cloves.

**2. Add the Wet Ingredients:** Stir in the water, oil, vanilla (if using), and glycerin (if using). Mix until combined.

**3. Cook the Dough:** Place the pot over medium heat and stir constantly. As the dough heats, it will begin to thicken. Continue stirring until it pulls away from the sides of the pot and forms a soft dough ball. It will take 3 to 5 minutes. Just be sure to stir during this time to prevent sticking or burning. As soon as it comes together into a ball, you can remove from the heat.

**4. Cool and Knead:** Let the dough cool for a few minutes, then knead on a flat surface until smooth and soft.

**5. Store:** Store the playdough in an airtight container or sealed plastic bag. It will stay soft for several weeks if stored properly.

# MORE *from* *the* GINGERBREAD KITCHEN

*Because there's always room for one more Christmas treat!*

# Christmas Gingerbread Cookie Box

*A Christmas cookie box, as shown on page 110, is one of the sweetest ways to share the season. I like to fill mine with a mix of flavors and textures: soft, spiced cookies like molasses sandwich cookies and gingerbread snowballs alongside cutouts, stamped chocolate cookies, and a few whimsical ones like reindeer and wreaths. For extra festive charm, I tuck in dried orange slices, cinnamon sticks, and candy canes to add fragrance and color.*

Use parchment paper or cupcake liners to separate delicate cookies, and be sure to let everything cool completely before boxing up. A mix of shapes and sizes keeps it visually interesting, and a simple ribbon or sprig of rosemary on top makes it feel extra special. Perfect for neighbors, teachers, or anyone who could use a little joy this time of year.

To make as pictured on page 110, see recipes for Gingerbread Men Cookies (page 50), Glazed Chocolate Gingerbread Stamp Cookies (page 114), Reindeer Gingersnap Cookies (page 117), Gingerbread Snowballs (page 122), Molasses Sandwich Cookies (page 125), and Gingerbread Wreath Cookies (page 126).

# Ginger Spice Tea

*This tea is like sipping a gingerbread cookie. It's warm, spiced, and full of flavor. It's such a treat on chilly December days, especially when served in your prettiest Christmas china.*

MAKES 1 SERVING

1 bag black tea

1 cup hot water

1 to 2 tablespoons Gingerbread Syrup (page 131)

Splash of warm milk, optional

Steep tea bag in hot water for 3 to 5 minutes. Stir in gingerbread syrup. Add a splash of warm milk, if desired.

### A SPOONFUL OF CHEER

Use the Gingerbread Men Cookies dough (page 50) to cut out spoon-shaped cookies. If you don't have a spoon-shaped cookie cutter, trace a demitasse or baby spoon onto card stock to create a template. Bake, tie each one with a red ribbon, and rest on the saucer beside each teacup. It's the sweetest little tea stirrer, and it tastes good too!

# Glazed Chocolate Gingerbread Stamp Cookies

*These stamped cookies are as beautiful as they are delicious. Cookie stamps date back centuries, with early versions carved from wood and passed down through the generations in Scandinavian and German families. I love collecting these charming molds and gifting them to friends tied with a bow. You can also use this dough for traditional cookie cutters too.*

MAKES 12 TO 14 COOKIES

½ cup unsalted butter, softened

⅓ cup packed dark brown sugar

2 tablespoons granulated sugar

¼ cup plus 2 tablespoons unsulfured molasses

1 large egg yolk

1 teaspoon vanilla extract

2 cups all-purpose flour

2 tablespoons Dutch-process cocoa powder

½ teaspoon baking soda

¾ teaspoon salt

2 teaspoons ground ginger

1 teaspoon ground cinnamon

½ teaspoon ground cloves

In the bowl of an electric mixer fitted with the paddle attachment, cream the butter, brown sugar, and granulated sugar on medium speed until light and fluffy, 2 to 3 minutes. Add the molasses, egg yolk, and vanilla, mixing until smooth and fully combined.

In a separate bowl, whisk together the flour, cocoa powder, baking soda, salt, ginger, cinnamon, and cloves.

With the mixer on low speed, gradually add the dry ingredients to the wet ingredients and mix just until a thick dough forms. Dough will be tacky, but should not be overly sticky. If so, add a tablespoon of flour.

Divide the dough in half and shape into two disks. Wrap each disk tightly in plastic wrap and refrigerate for at least 2 hours. Chill the cookie stamps as well; cold stamps create the sharpest impressions.

Preheat the oven to 350 degrees F.

On a lightly floured silicone baking mat or sheet of parchment paper, roll out the chilled dough to ¼-inch thickness. Dust the surface lightly with flour and smooth it across the surface. Firmly press the chilled cookie stamp into the dough, then lift up and repeat. Be sure both the dough and stamp remain well chilled to keep the impressions crisp. Repeat with remaining dough. Transfer the entire mat or sheet of parchment paper onto a baking sheet. Bake for 8 to 9 minutes, or until the edges are set and the centers are just firm. Be careful not to overbake; these cookies are best when they stay soft. Let cool completely before glazing.

### FOR THE GLAZE

1 cup powdered sugar, sifted

1 tablespoon unsalted butter, melted

1 teaspoon vanilla extract

1 to 2 tablespoons milk or heavy cream

Pinch of salt

To make the glaze, whisk together the powdered sugar, melted butter, vanilla, milk, and salt until smooth. Use a pastry brush to apply the glaze to each stamped cookie, wiping away any excess so the design stays visible.

#### *Stamp Cookie Tips*

Store the cookie stamps in the refrigerator. The cold stamp helps prevent the dough from sticking.

Instead of rolling out the dough, you can also roll individual 1-inch balls of dough and then press each down with the cookie stamp.

If the dough begins to stick, lightly flour the stamp before pressing (lightly tap off excess).

# Reindeer Gingersnap Cookies

*These gingersnaps are delicious all on their own, but add chocolate antlers, eyes, and a candy nose, and they transform into the cutest little reindeer treats. Perfect for cookie boxes, Christmas cookie exchanges, or a cozy family baking night!*

MAKES 24 GINGERSNAP COOKIES

10 tablespoons (1 stick plus 2 tablespoons) unsalted butter, softened

1 cup granulated sugar

¼ cup unsulfured molasses

1 large egg, room temperature

2 ½ cups all-purpose flour

1 ½ teaspoons ground ginger

1 teaspoon ground cinnamon

½ teaspoon ground cloves

½ teaspoon baking soda

¼ teaspoon salt

In the bowl of a stand mixer fitted with the paddle attachment (or using a hand mixer), cream together the butter and sugar on medium speed until light and fluffy, 2 to 3 minutes. Add the molasses and egg, mixing until smooth. Scrape down the bowl to ensure everything is fully incorporated.

In a separate bowl, whisk together the flour, ginger, cinnamon, cloves, baking soda, and salt. With the mixer on low, gradually add the dry ingredients to the wet ingredients until combined. Dough will be soft and slightly sticky.

Divide the dough into two disks, wrap tightly in plastic wrap, and refrigerate for at least 2 hours or overnight.

When ready to bake, preheat the oven to 350 degrees F. On a lightly floured surface, roll out the dough very thinly (about ⅛ inch). Cut into circles using a 2½-inch round cutter and place on silicone baking mats or baking sheets lined with parchment paper. Roll the dough directly on parchment paper or a baking mat so you can peel away the excess and transfer the whole thing to a baking sheet easily.

Bake for 8 to 10 minutes, or until the edges are slightly darker. The cookies will crisp as they cool.

## REINDEER DETAILS

½ cup chocolate chips or chocolate wafers, for melting

Red Mini M&M's

Melt chocolate in a microwave-safe bowl until smooth, then transfer to a small piping bag and snip the corner. Pipe antlers onto each cookie. Add small dots of chocolate for the eyes and another small dot of chocolate to attach a red Mini M&M for the nose. Let the cookies set completely before serving or packaging.

# Apple Gingerbread Loaf

*I love baking these loaves when we have company in town. It makes the whole house smell like Christmas. I slice one for breakfast and wrap the other up with Christmas ribbon to send home with guests.*

MAKES 2 MEDIUM (4 X 8-INCH) LOAVES

2 cups all-purpose flour

2 teaspoons ground cinnamon

1½ teaspoons ground ginger

½ teaspoon ground cloves

½ teaspoon nutmeg

1 teaspoon baking soda

½ teaspoon baking powder

½ teaspoon salt

¼ cup vegetable oil

¼ cup melted butter, slightly cooled

½ cup packed dark brown sugar

½ cup granulated sugar

½ cup unsulfured molasses

2 large eggs

½ cup unsweetened applesauce

⅓ cup sour cream or plain Greek yogurt

2 teaspoons vanilla extract

1 large apple, diced (about 1½ cups)

Preheat the oven to 350 degrees F. Lightly grease or line two 8 x 4-inch loaf pans with parchment paper.

In a medium bowl, whisk together the flour, cinnamon, ginger, cloves, nutmeg, baking soda, baking powder, and salt.

In a large mixing bowl, whisk together the oil, melted butter, brown sugar, granulated sugar, and molasses until smooth. Add the eggs, applesauce, sour cream, and vanilla. Whisk until fully combined.

Add the dry ingredients to the wet ingredients, stirring gently until just combined. Do not overmix. Fold in the diced apples.

Divide the batter evenly between the prepared loaf pans and smooth the tops.

Bake for 40 to 50 minutes, or until a toothpick inserted in the center comes out with a few moist crumbs (not wet batter). Ovens vary, so watch carefully. Tent with aluminum foil toward the end if the tops begin to brown too quickly.

# Spiced Gingerbread Pecans

*One thing I could always count on at my grandparents' upstate South Carolina home during the holidays was a big bowl of candied pecans. I make a big batch of these every December, they're just that versatile. I use them in my Spiced Pecan and Brie Puff Pastry Bites (page 70), serve them in little silver bowls at Christmas gatherings, and tuck them into gift bags for neighbors and friends.*

MAKES APPROXIMATELY 3 CUPS

1 egg white

1 tablespoon water

1 teaspoon vanilla extract

3 cups pecan halves

½ cup dark brown sugar

2 tablespoons granulated sugar

1½ teaspoons cinnamon

½ teaspoon ground ginger

¼ teaspoon nutmeg

¼ teaspoon cloves

¾ teaspoon salt

Preheat the oven to 300 degrees F.

In a large mixing bowl, whisk the egg white and water until frothy. Stir in the vanilla. Add the pecans and toss until fully coated.

In a separate bowl, stir together the brown sugar, granulated sugar, cinnamon, ginger, nutmeg, cloves, and salt. Sprinkle the mixture over the pecans and toss again until evenly coated.

Spread the pecans in a single layer on a baking sheet lined with a silicone baking mat, or directly on an unlined sheet lightly coated with nonstick spray.

Bake for 25 to 30 minutes, stirring halfway through, until toasted and fragrant.

Once cooled, store the pecans in an airtight container at room temperature. I keep mine in a large tin just like my grandparents did, but any lidded container or glass jar works well. They'll stay fresh for up to 2 weeks, if they last that long! They also freeze beautifully.

*Baking Tip:* I don't recommend parchment paper for this recipe, because the nuts can stick. A silicone baking mat or greased baking sheet works best.

# Gingerbread Snowballs

*A twist on the classic pecan snowballs my mom made every Christmas, this gingerbread-spiced version is melt-in-your-mouth and coated in just the right dusting of powdered sugar "snow." I love serving them in a pretty antique silver dish or wrapping them up to gift during the season.*

MAKES 36 SNOWBALLS

1 cup (2 sticks) unsalted butter, softened

½ cup powdered sugar, plus more for rolling

2 teaspoons vanilla extract

2 tablespoons unsulfured molasses

2 cups all-purpose flour

1½ teaspoons ground cinnamon

1 teaspoon ground ginger

¼ teaspoon ground cloves

¼ teaspoon nutmeg

¼ teaspoon salt

Preheat the oven to 350 degrees F. Line a baking sheet with parchment paper or a silicone baking mat.

In the bowl of a stand mixer fitted with the paddle attachment, cream the softened butter and powdered sugar on medium speed until light and fluffy. Add the vanilla and molasses and mix until fully incorporated, pausing to scrape down the sides of the bowl.

In a separate bowl, whisk together the flour, cinnamon, ginger, cloves, nutmeg, and salt. With the mixer on low speed, gradually add the dry ingredients to the wet ingredients until a soft dough forms.

Roll the dough into 1-inch balls and place on the prepared baking sheet, spacing about 1 inch apart.

Bake for 11 to 13 minutes or until the bottoms are just golden and the tops look set. Let the cookies cool for about 5 minutes, until they're just cool enough to handle, then roll in powdered sugar.

Once fully cooled, roll a second time for the full snowball effect.

# Molasses Sandwich Cookies

*These soft, spiced molasses cookies are perfectly delicious on their own, but I like to make them extra special with a swirl of cinnamon buttercream sandwiched in between. Supposedly, they're a huge hit with Santa too.*

MAKES 24 COOKIES

½ cup unsalted butter, room temperature

1 cup granulated sugar

1 large egg

¼ cup unsulfured molasses

2 teaspoons vanilla extract

2 cups all-purpose flour

¼ teaspoon salt

1 teaspoon ground cinnamon

½ teaspoon ground cloves

½ teaspoon ground ginger

¼ teaspoon ground nutmeg

1½ teaspoons baking soda

½ cup coarse sparkling sugar

Preheat the oven to 350 degrees F and line a baking sheet with parchment paper. Set aside.

In the bowl of a stand mixer fitted with the paddle attachment (or with a hand mixer), cream together the butter and sugar until light and fluffy, 3 to 4 minutes.

Add the egg and mix until combined. Add the molasses and vanilla and beat again until fully incorporated.

In a separate mixing bowl, whisk together the flour, salt, cinnamon, cloves, ginger, nutmeg, and baking soda.

Gradually add the dry ingredients to the wet ingredients, mixing until a sticky dough forms.

The dough will be soft and sticky; this is normal. You can use a little flour on your hands to help roll into 1- to 2-inch balls. Roll the dough balls in coarse sparkling sugar for a sparkly finish.

Place on the prepared baking sheet and bake for 10 to 12 minutes, just until the cookies are set. Be careful not to overbake.

Let the cookies cool completely before assembling.

## CINNAMON BUTTERCREAM

1 cup unsalted butter, room temperature

3 cups powdered sugar

2 teaspoons ground cinnamon

1 teaspoon vanilla extract

2 tablespoons milk or heavy cream, plus more as needed

Pinch of salt

In the bowl of a stand mixer fitted with the paddle attachment (or using a hand mixer), beat the butter on medium speed until smooth and creamy, 1 to 2 minutes. Add the powdered sugar, cinnamon, vanilla, milk, and salt. Mix on low speed until combined, then increase to medium and beat for 2 to 3 minutes, until light and fluffy.

Transfer the buttercream to a piping bag fitted with a fluted tip. Pipe a swirl onto the flat side of one cookie, then gently press a second cookie on top to sandwich it. Store in an airtight container.

# Gingerbread Wreath Cookies

*These charming little wreaths start with the same dough as my classic Gingerbread Men Cookies, but get a festive twist with a glaze, chopped rosemary, and tiny mint leaves to resemble greenery and a bow. They're one of my favorite cookies to style on a holiday dessert table.*

MAKES APPROXIMATELY 24 WREATH COOKIES

¾ cup (1½ sticks) unsalted butter

½ cup packed dark brown sugar

¼ cup granulated sugar

¾ cup unsulfured molasses

2 teaspoons vanilla extract

1 tablespoon heavy cream or whole milk

1 teaspoon salt

1 tablespoon ground cinnamon

2 teaspoons ground ginger

¼ teaspoon ground nutmeg

¼ teaspoon ground cloves

1 large egg, room temperature

3½ to 4 cups all-purpose flour

½ teaspoon baking soda

### WREATH DECORATING GLAZE

1 cup powdered sugar, sifted

2 to 3 tablespoons milk

1 teaspoon vanilla extract

Rosemary, mint leaves, red nonpareils, and coarse sparkling sugar, for decorating

In a medium saucepan (or microwave-safe bowl), melt the butter over low heat. Remove from the heat and stir in the brown sugar, granulated sugar, molasses, vanilla, cream, salt, and spices. Whisk until smooth.

Transfer the mixture to a large mixing bowl and let it cool to lukewarm. Beat in the egg.

In a separate bowl, whisk together the flour and baking soda. Gradually stir the dry ingredients into the wet ingredients until a soft dough forms. Start with 3½ cups flour; if the dough feels too sticky add more, a couple of tablespoons at a time.

Divide the dough in half, pat each portion into a thick rectangle, wrap tightly in plastic wrap, and refrigerate for at least 1 hour.

Preheat the oven to 350 degrees F. Roll the dough out directly onto parchment paper or a silicone baking mat to ¼-inch thickness. Use a larger fluted round cutter for the outer shape and a smaller round cutter for the center to form a wreath. Peel away the excess dough around each wreath and transfer the full sheet to a baking sheet to keep their shape intact.

Chill the cut-out wreaths on the baking sheet for 5 to 10 minutes before baking.

Bake for 6 to 8 minutes, until just set.

Whisk together the powdered sugar, milk, and vanilla until smooth. Brush or spoon over wreath cookies and set on a wire rack. Sprinkle with chopped fresh rosemary. Add tiny mint leaves and red nonpareils to mimic holly leaves and berries. Finish with a sprinkling of coarse sparkling sugar. Let the glaze dry completely before storing or stacking.

*Candy Twist:* Instead of mint leaves, you can also roll a green gumdrop thin with a rolling pin and cut out small leaf shapes.

# Orange Gingerbread Cinnamon Rolls

*Orange rolls were always a favorite of mine growing up, and I've always loved infusing citrus into baked goods, especially at Christmastime. The orange in these rolls pairs beautifully with the cozy spices of gingerbread, making this one of my very favorite recipes and a true holiday staple. They're soft, ooey gooey, and my husband's hands-down favorite.*

MAKES 12 TO 14 LARGE ROLLS

## FOR THE DOUGH

1 cup warm whole milk (110 to 115 degrees F)

1 tablespoon instant yeast

½ cup granulated sugar

2 tablespoons molasses

⅓ cup unsalted butter, softened

2 large eggs, room temperature

4 ½ cups all-purpose flour

1 teaspoon salt

2 teaspoons ground ginger

½ teaspoon ground cinnamon

¼ teaspoon ground cloves, optional

Stir the warm milk and yeast together in the mixing bowl, cover with a clean towel, and let it sit for 5 to 10 minutes. If it doesn't foam, the yeast is likely expired and should be replaced, or the milk was too hot and killed the yeast.

In the bowl of a stand mixer fitted with the paddle attachment, combine the foamy yeast mixture (or just the warm milk and yeast), sugar, molasses, softened butter, and eggs. Mix until mostly smooth.

Add the flour, salt, and spices. Mix until just combined, then switch to the dough hook and knead on medium-low speed for 5 to 6 minutes. The dough should be slightly tacky but not wet.

Transfer the dough to a lightly greased bowl. Cover and let rise in a warm spot until doubled in size, 45 to 60 minutes. I often let mine go a little longer if the kitchen is cool or I want an extra fluffy roll. Just be sure the dough has puffed up noticeably before moving on.

*Rising Tips:* Kitchens can be chilly in December, which can slow down the rising time. If the dough needs a warmer spot, try placing the bowl near a sunny window. A warm dryer, heating vent, or even a microwave with a mug of hot water inside can also create a cozy spot. Just be sure it's warm, not hot.

*Continued* ➝

### FOR THE FILLING

⅓ cup unsalted butter, melted

1 cup packed brown sugar

1 ½ tablespoons ground cinnamon

1 ½ teaspoons ground ginger

1 tablespoon molasses

1 teaspoon orange zest

Pinch of salt

### TO SPREAD ON ROLLED DOUGH

¼ cup unsalted butter, softened

While the dough rises, stir together the melted butter, brown sugar, cinnamon, ginger, molasses, zest, and salt for the filling.

Roll the dough out into a 16 x 21-inch rectangle. Spread the surface with the softened butter, then evenly sprinkle on the filling. Roll up tightly starting at a long edge and slice into 12 to 14 rolls.

Place the rolls into a greased 9 x 13-inch baking dish. Cover loosely and let rise again until puffy, 30 to 45 minutes.

Preheat the oven to 350 degrees F. Bake the rolls uncovered for 18 to 22 minutes, until golden brown and baked through.

### FOR THE CREAM CHEESE FROSTING

3 ounces cream cheese, softened

¼ cup unsalted butter, softened

1 ½ cups powdered sugar

½ teaspoon vanilla extract

1 tablespoon fresh orange juice

⅛ teaspoon salt

Orange zest, for garnish

While the rolls are baking, beat the cream cheese and butter together until smooth. Add the powdered sugar, vanilla, orange juice, salt, and zest and mix until fluffy and spreadable.

Spread the frosting on the warm cinnamon rolls and garnish with orange zest.

#### *Christmas Morning Tip*

Planning for Christmas morning? Prep the rolls on Christmas Eve, just up to the point where they've been rolled and placed in the 9 x 13-inch baking pan. Cover tightly and refrigerate overnight. In the morning, let the rolls rest in a warm spot for 45 to 60 minutes while the oven preheats. Once they've puffed up, bake as directed.

By the time little feet are running down the stairs to check for signs of Santa, your kitchen will smell like gingerbread spice!

# Gingerbread Syrup

*This cozy syrup is the secret behind our Gingerbread Martini (page 69) and Ginger Spice Tea (page 112), but it doesn't stop there. It's also delicious stirred into coffee, drizzled over pound cake, or packaged up in a pretty jar for a sweet homemade gift.*

MAKES 1 ¼ CUPS SYRUP

1 cup water

1 cup dark brown sugar

⅓ cup molasses

1 teaspoon cinnamon

½ teaspoon cloves

¼ teaspoon nutmeg

2 teaspoons ground ginger (or ½ cup fresh ginger, cut into 1-inch pieces)

1 teaspoon vanilla extract

Add all ingredients except the vanilla to a small saucepan and whisk to combine. Bring to a gentle boil over medium-high heat, then reduce to a simmer over medium-low heat. Let it simmer for 7 to 8 minutes, whisking occasionally, until the mixture has slightly thickened.

Remove from the heat and stir in the vanilla. Strain the syrup through a fine mesh sieve if desired.

Allow to cool completely, then transfer to an airtight container. Store in the refrigerator for 1 to 2 weeks.

*Note:* This syrup is meant to be pourable, like a simple syrup. For a thicker syrup, simmer 1 to 2 minutes longer or reduce water slightly.

# Gingerbread House Cookie Decorating Board

*Think of this cookie board like a gingerbread-inspired charcuterie board! Perfect for parties, family gatherings, or even traveling (no collapsing houses here!). Just bake house-shaped cookies, set out a few bowls of icing and candy, and let everyone decorate their own gingerbread house without the pressure of building a full 3D house. Let your creativity run wild decorating these gingerbread cookie houses, but most of all, have fun!*

## FOR THE COOKIES

Prepare 1 batch of dough for Gingerbread Men Cookies (page 50).

Roll the dough to ¼-inch thickness on parchment paper or a silicone baking mat. Use house-shaped cookie cutters to create your gingerbread houses. For windows and doors, use small rectangular cutters and small round cutters (or even the back of a piping tip). You can also simply pipe them on with icing.

Transfer the full piece of parchment paper to a baking sheet to preserve the shapes. Freeze the cutouts for 5 to 10 minutes, then bake at 350 degrees F for 6 to 8 minutes or until just set. Cool completely before decorating.

**Variation:** You can also use a sugar cookie dough designed for cutouts if you prefer. Just be sure it's a no-spread recipe so the house shapes keep their crisp edges while baking.

## FOR DECORATING

Gingerbread House Royal Icing (page 41)

Food coloring gel for tinting icing, optional

Assorted candies: peppermints, gumdrops, rainbow sprinkles, red hots, mini candy canes, chewy fruit slices, M&M's, etc.

Mini marshmallows (or large ones cut into small pieces)

Rosemary sprigs, for garnish

Divide icing into bowls and tint as desired. Spoon into piping bags fitted with small round or star tips.

**Icing Note:** You can use either Gingerbread House Royal Icing (page 41) or a traditional buttercream. Royal icing will harden as it dries, which is helpful if you plan to stack or transport the cookies. Buttercream stays soft, so it's best for cookies that will be enjoyed the same day or displayed flat.

## TO SERVE

Arrange cookies on a large board or tray, surrounded by bowls of icing and candies. Tuck rosemary sprigs around the edges for greenery and add twinkle lights for extra sparkle.

# TEMPLATE PATTERNS

## CLASSIC GINGERBREAD HOUSE

Classic Gingerbread House templates are 2⁄5 size. Copy or scan at 250% to use at full size.

> *Note:* Measurement notes on all templates are for the final sizing.

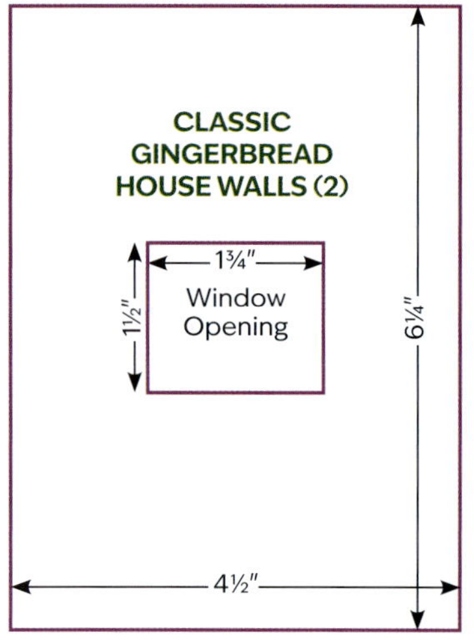


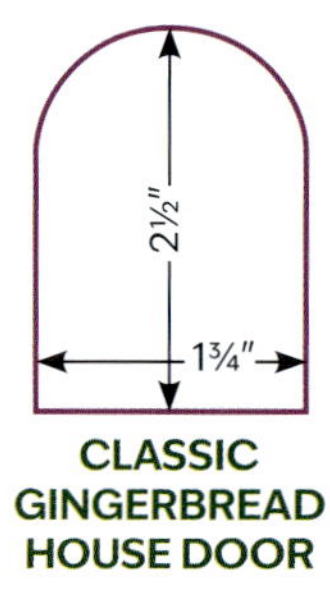


CLASSIC GINGERBREAD HOUSE DOOR

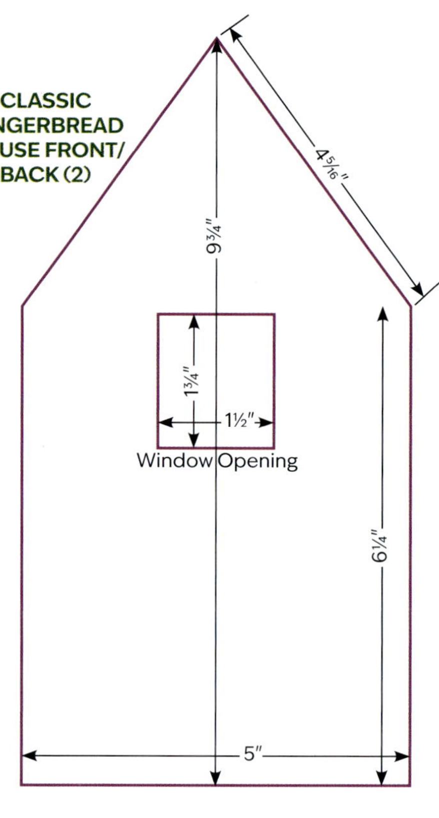


CLASSIC GINGERBREAD HOUSE BOTTOM (2)

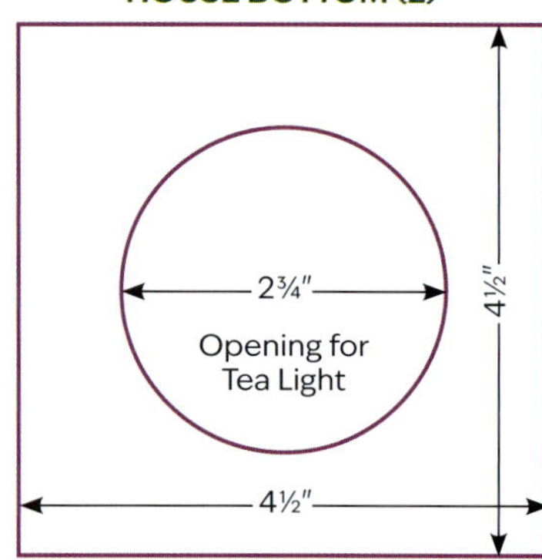


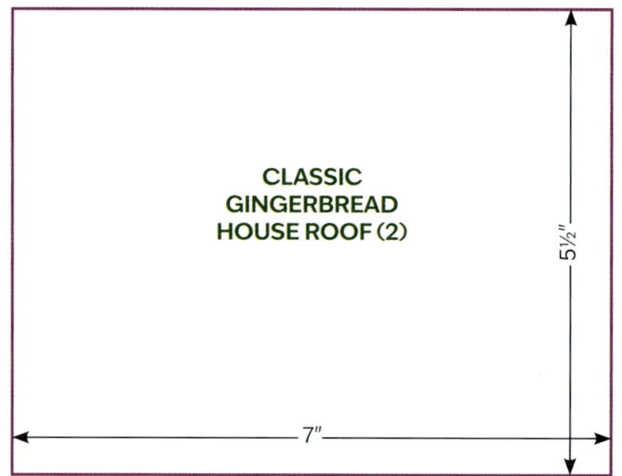

## INDIVIDUAL TRAIN

Individual Train templates are ½ size. Copy or scan at 200% to use at full size.

*Note:* Measurement notes on all templates are for the final sizing.

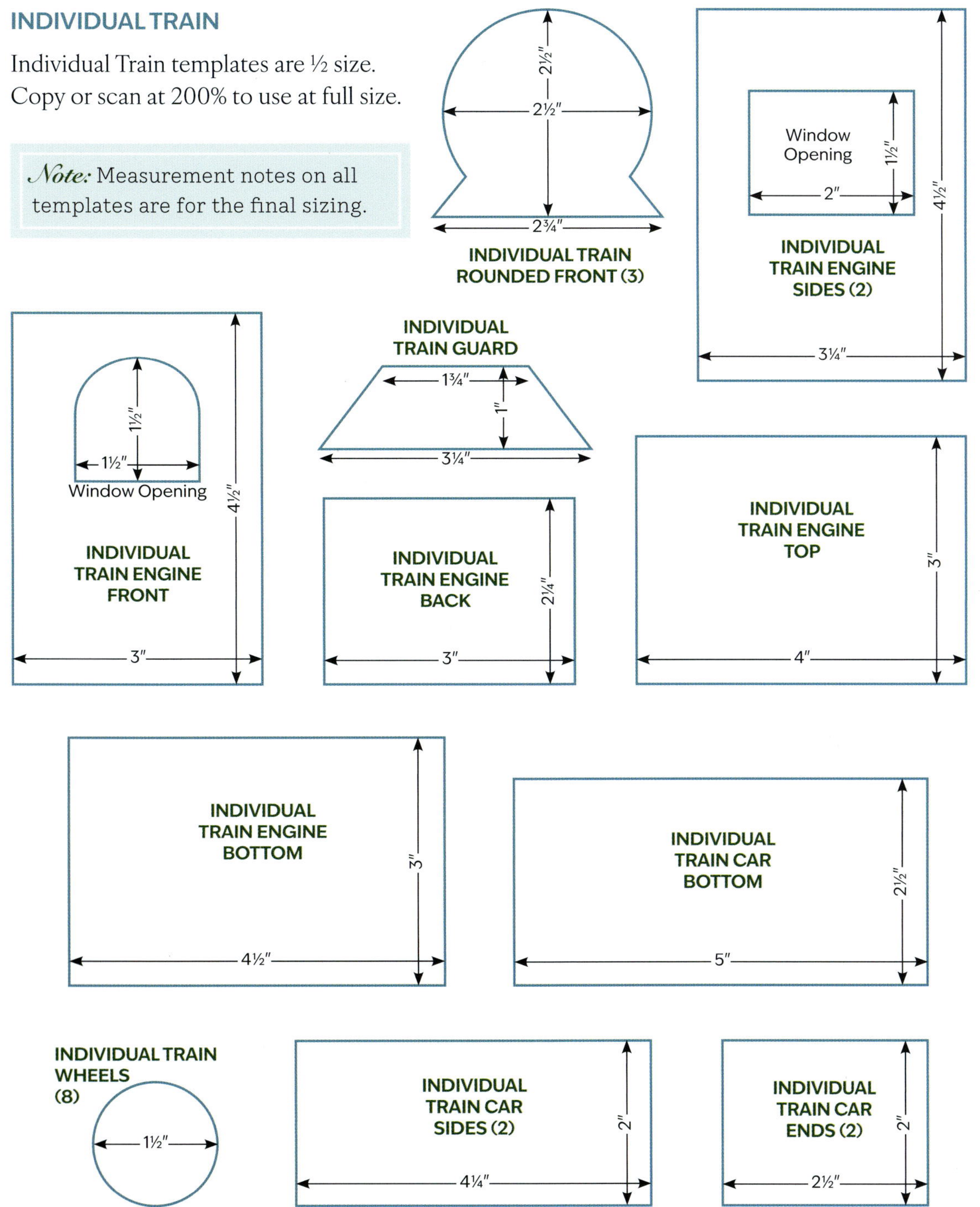

## LARGE CENTERPIECE TRAIN

Large Train templates are ⅓ size. Copy or scan at 300% to use at full size.

*Note:* Measurement notes on all templates are for the final sizing.

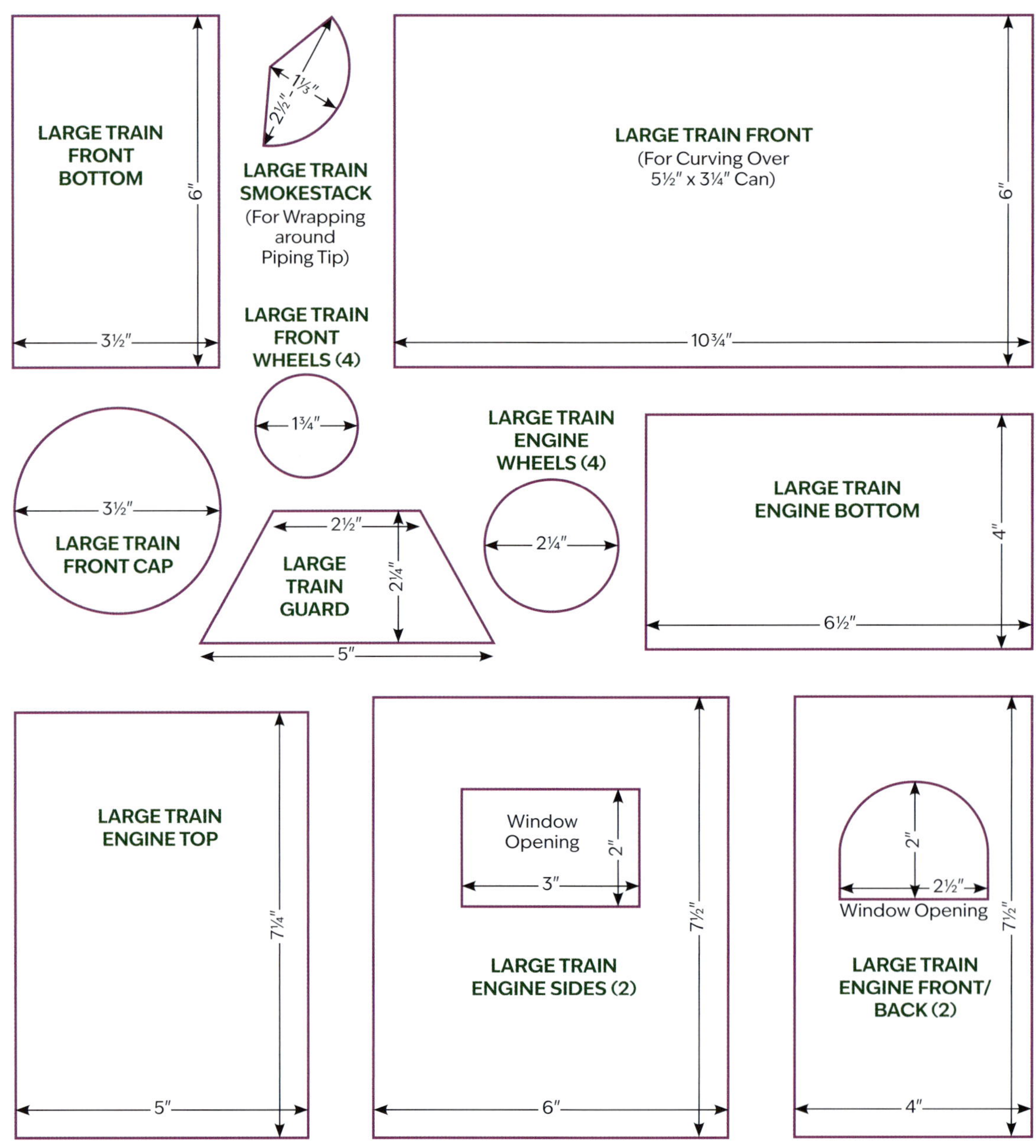

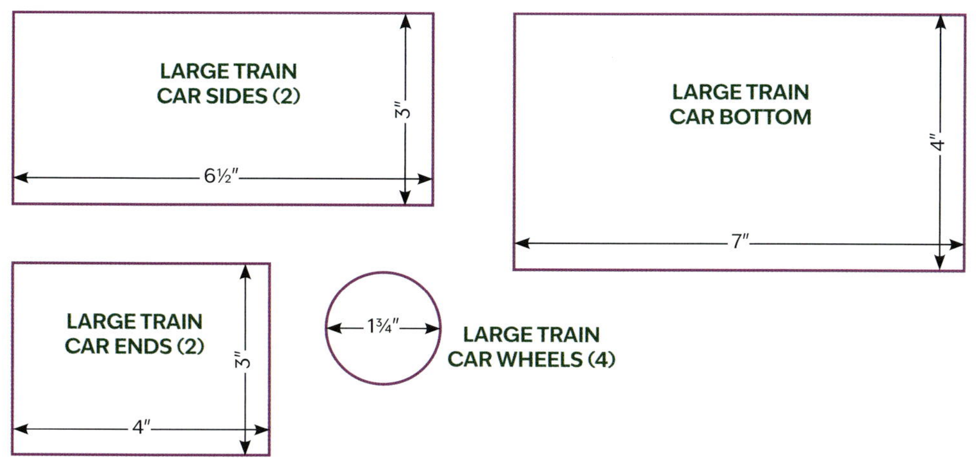


## GINGERBREAD COTTAGE

Gingerbread Cottage templates are ½ size. Copy or scan at 200% to use at full size.

*Note:* Measurement notes on all templates are for the final sizing.

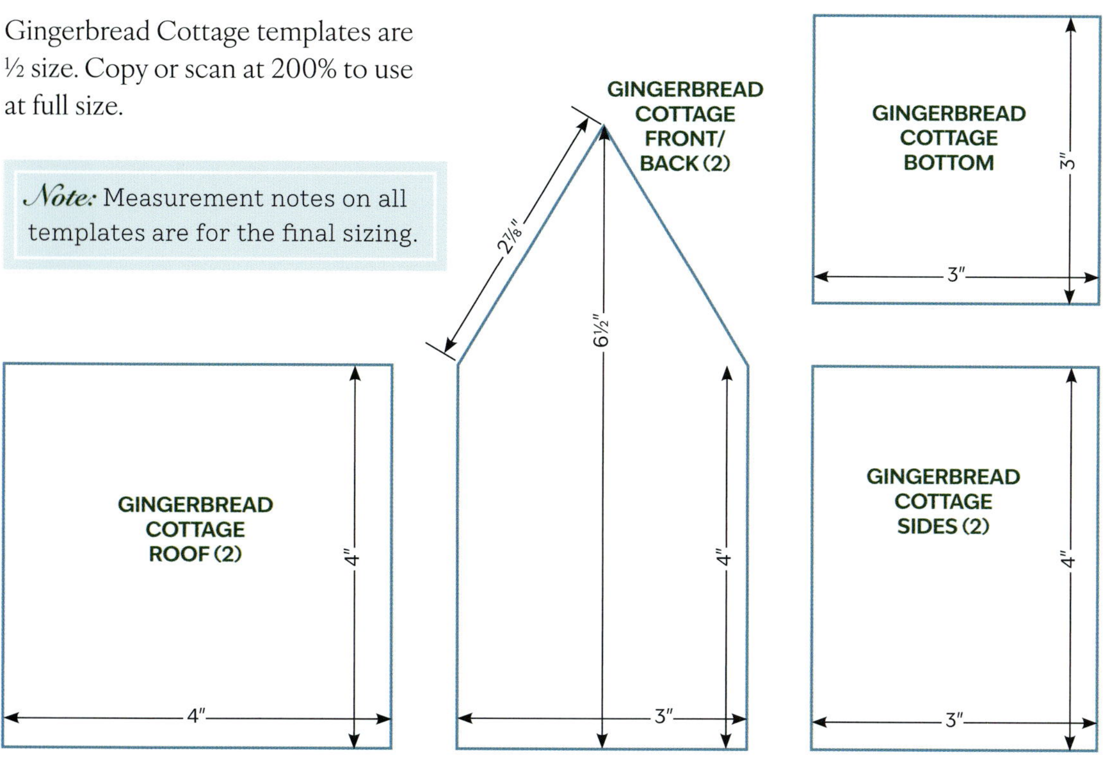

## PETITE GINGERBREAD HOUSE

Petite Gingerbread House templates are full size.

*Note:* Measurement notes on all templates are for the final sizing.

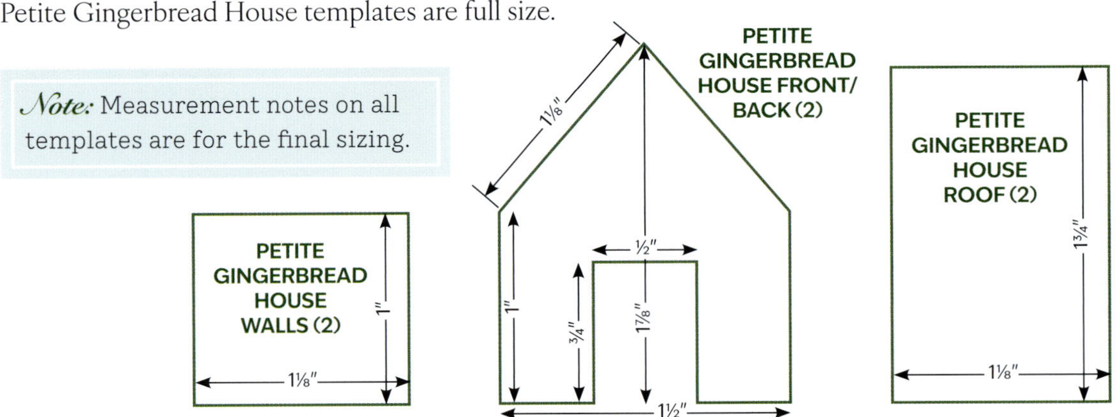


## GINGERBREAD SLEIGHS

Large and Small Sleigh templates are ⅔ size. Copy or scan at 150% to use at full size.

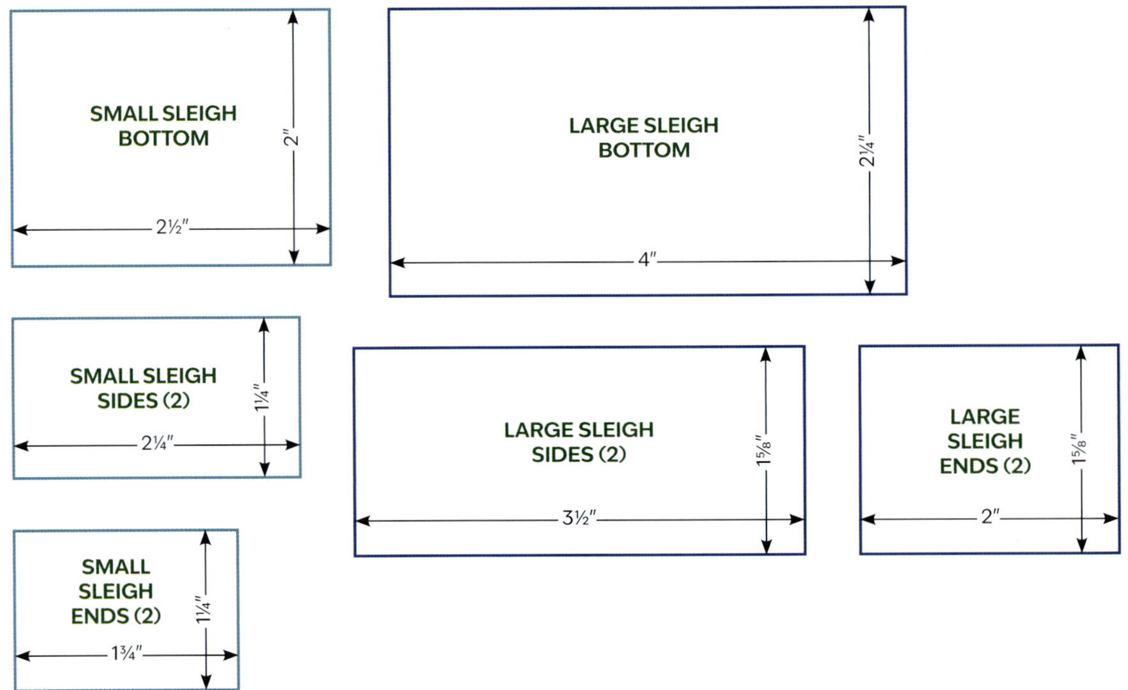

# ACKNOWLEDGMENTS

Heartfelt thanks to Cameron Wilder for capturing the magic so beautifully. You are a true talent and a joy to work with. To my husband Chris, thank you for your constant help and encouragement, in more ways than I can count. Blakely and Ivy, your excitement for this tradition each year (and your very enthusiastic taste-testing!) made creating this book all the more special. Thank you to Rinne Sade for your thoughtful support, and to Michelle Branson and the entire Gibbs Smith team for believing in this book and bringing it to life. Jessica Evans, I'm so grateful for your constant encouragement and true friendship. And to Michael and Patrick Evans, you added the perfect touch of holiday charm.

And finally, to the thousands of you who join in each Christmas, watching, cheering, and creating your own gingerbread house traditions inspired by our annual tea party, thank you. Your enthusiasm and kind messages over the years are the reason this book exists. We are endlessly grateful.

# INDEX

# METRIC CONVERSION CHART

| VOLUME MEASUREMENTS | | WEIGHT MEASUREMENTS | | TEMPERATURE CONVERSION | |
|---|---|---|---|---|---|
| U.S. | METRIC | U.S. | METRIC | FAHRENHEIT | CELSIUS |
| 1 teaspoon | 5 ml | ½ ounce | 15 g | 250 | 120 |
| 1 tablespoon | 15 ml | 1 ounce | 30 g | 300 | 150 |
| ¼ cup | 60 ml | 3 ounces | 90 g | 325 | 160 |
| ⅓ cup | 75 ml | 4 ounces | 115 g | 350 | 177 |
| ½ cup | 125 ml | 8 ounces | 225 g | 375 | 190 |
| ⅔ cup | 150 ml | 12 ounces | 350 g | 400 | 200 |
| ¾ cup | 175 ml | 1 pound | 450 g | 425 | 220 |
| 1 cup | 250 ml | 2 ¼ pounds | 1 kg | 450 | 230 |

*Courtney Dial Whitmore* is the author of the best-selling *The Southern Entertainer's Cookbook* and four other books on food and entertaining. She founded Pizzazzerie.com, where her festive recipes and creative entertaining ideas have been featured by *Southern Living*, HGTV, *Better Homes & Gardens*, and Martha Stewart. Courtney lives in Charleston, South Carolina, with her husband and their two daughters, Blakely and Ivy. She and her mother, Phronsie Horton Dial, work side by side in Charleston, sharing a lifelong passion for celebrating life's sweetest traditions. Writing this book together has been a dream many years in the making, one that finally brings the magic of gingerbread and Christmas to life.

*Cameron Wilder* is a lifestyle and editorial photographer focused on helping individuals and brands create imagery that resonates and tells their story in an authentic way. His work has been featured in the pages of *Southern Living*, *Garden & Gun*, *Vogue*, *Condé Nast Traveler*, and more. He loves getting to work with creative people with big ideas, which is why he was so thrilled to collaborate with Courtney on this book and enter into her beautiful world of gingerbread and holiday entertaining. A native South Carolinian, Cameron lives in Charleston with his wife, Tolly, and son, Brooks. After shooting this book, he is more prepared than ever to win his family's annual gingerbread competition.